Canada: Our Home

THE MACMILLAN ELEMENTARY SOCIAL STUDIES PROGRAM

Project Five to Nine (Teacher's Resource Book) by Peter Harper et al.

Canada: Our Roots and Environment (CORE), Barry Griffiths, General Editor

Canada: Immigrants and Settlers by Ian Hundey

Canada: Builders of the Nation by Ian Hundey

The Macmillan School Atlas by Ronald C. Daly

Canada: Our Roots and Environment (CORE)

GENERAL EDITOR

Barry Griffiths, Principal, Gulfstream Public School, North York
Board of Education, Ontario

SERIES CONSULTANTS

Derek Hounsell, Principal, W. E. Cormack Academy,
Stephenville, Newfoundland
Richard L. Wray, Social Studies Consultant, Edmonton Catholic
School District, Alberta

AUTHORS

J. M. Daly   John D. Jeneroux
E. Anne Gibson   E. C. Pickles
Barry Griffiths   R. W. Trueman

TITLES

Canada: Our Home
Canada: Our People
Canada: Our Heritage
Canada: Our Place in the World

Canada: Our Home

Barry Griffiths
Principal, Gulfstream Public School
North York, Ontario

J. M. Daly
Principal, St. Paul Separate School
Kingston, Ontario

MACMILLAN OF CANADA
A Canadian Company

Cover art by Sylvie Daigneault.

Illustration acknowledgments are on page 186.

Canadian Cataloguing in Publication Data

Griffiths, Barry, date
  Canada, our home

(Canada, our roots and environment)

ISBN 0-7705-1781-1

1. Canada — Social conditions — 1965-   *
2. Canada — Social life and customs — 1965-   *
I. Daly, James M., date. II. Title. III. Series.

FC57.G75   971.064   C79-094915-6
F1008.2.G75

Printed in Canada for
The Macmillan Company of Canada Limited
70 Bond Street, Toronto, Ontario M5B 1X3
Affiliated with Maclean-Hunter Limited

Contents

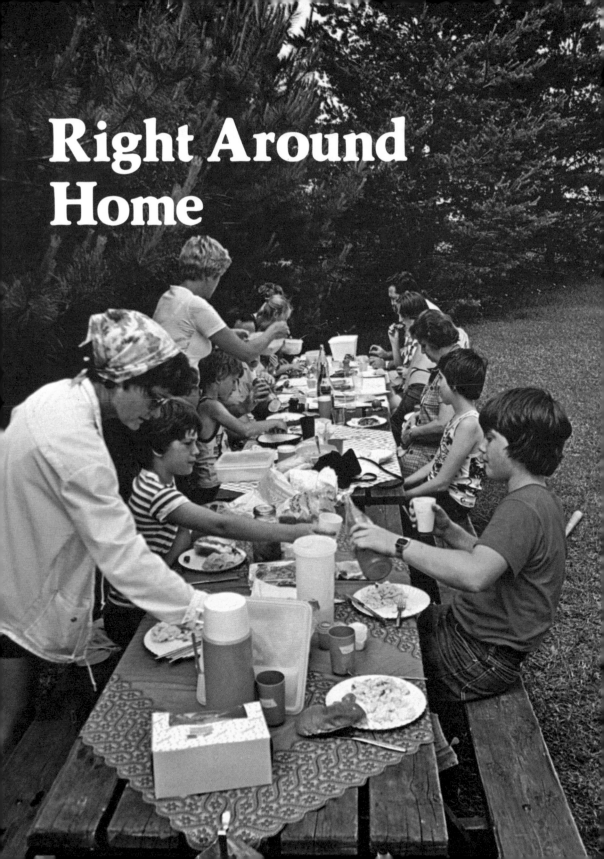

Right Around Home

1 Let's Build a Tree House

The Big Idea

Greg got up early. He just couldn't stay in bed. This was Tuesday, a special day. He wanted to be first into the tree house! Quickly he pulled on his clothes, tugging at the sweater.

In the kitchen he put some cereal into a bowl and poured a glass of juice. He tried to be quiet. He didn't want to wake up the family.

As he sat at the table, Greg remembered how it had all started. That was a week ago.

Greg and his friends, Rob and Paul, had been out at the back of the house.

"What do you want to do?" asked Rob.

Everyone had some ideas, but none seemed very interesting. The boys began to walk toward the back of the yard where the large trees stood. Rob swung on the gate, while the others leaned on the fence.

"What we need is a place of our own—one that is really our own!"

They thought for a minute.

"A tent," someone said.

"A fort?"

"I know—a tree house!"

That seemed like the best idea. But now they had a problem. How do you build a tree house?

▶ 1. Find these things in the picture map of Greg's neighbourhood.
   (a) an apple tree
   (b) a fence with a gate in it
   (c) a dog pen
   (d) a one-storey house
   (e) the woods
   (f) a fire hydrant
   (g) a two-storey house
   (h) a vegetable garden
   (i) a tool shed

▶ 2. (a) Where is the tallest tree?
   (b) Which fence is longer, the fence at the back of Greg's
       garden or the one at the side?

     (c) Which house is taller, Number 10 or Number 12?

     (d) Which house is wider, Number 12 or Number 14?

     (e) Which house is closer to Number 12, Number 10 or Number 14?

▶ 3. Which part of the neighbourhood is flat? Which part is hilly?

▶ 4. Follow these directions.

     (a) Imagine you are standing in the driveway of Greg's house, Number 12. Face Greg's house.

     (b) Turn right and walk until you come to a fence.

     (c) Turn left at the fence. Walk to the end of the yard.

     (d) Now turn left again. What can you see in front of you?

     (e) Make up your own directions. Tell how you go from the gate to the front door of Number 14.

The first thing to do was to look for a good tree. A tree house couldn't be built in just any old tree. The three boys started to climb.

"These branches are sure strong," said Paul. "They don't even bend when you stand on them."

A yell from Greg made them all look up.

"Hey, look what I've found—a robin's nest. The eggs are still warm."

Rob shook his head. "We can't use this tree. The robins beat us to it. Let's try another."

Soon, all three agreed on the tree for their house. It was a big maple with thick, strong branches.

Back on the ground, Paul remembered a TV show he had seen. A group of children had built a tree house. He told his friends what it had been like.

As he talked, the boys kept adding new ideas.

"Let's have a blue door."

"How about a rope ladder?"

"And a window. It has to have a window."

"A sign, too—BEWARE! PRIVATE!"

"Let's stop dreaming and get to work," said Greg. "I want to get started."

"I'll ask my mom for a hammer and a saw," Greg called back. He was already running.

"My dad has some wood in the garage," said Paul. "It's left over from that fence he built last year."

The two boys ran over to Paul's house. They came back with their arms full of wood. They threw it in a pile beside the gate.

Rob and Paul were excited. They talked about their tree house.

"It's just for us. Nobody else," said Rob.

"We'll eat our sandwiches up there." Paul looked up into the tree. "Wow. Maybe we can even sleep up there."

"Hooray! Here comes Greg with the tools."

Greg picked a plank from the pile. He began to saw.
The other two watched. Soon Greg was too tired to go
on. They took turns. It took a long time to saw through
the wood.

"What do we do now?" Paul wanted to know.

Nobody answered.

▶ 1. Why have the boys run into problems with their tree house?

▶ 2. How would you go about building a tree house?

▶ 3. (a) Why do you think Rob said, "It's just for us. Nobody
else"?
    (b) If it were your tree house, would you feel the same way?
    Why, or why not?

▶ 4. Paul said, "What do we do now?" What ideas would you give
him?

▶ 5. Is it better to have one person try to solve a problem, or several people? Why?

"We're in trouble," said Greg. "We don't know how to build a tree house." The others agreed. They sat down and looked at the pile of wood.

"Maybe we need some help," said Paul. "My sister is home. She has good ideas sometimes."

They thought for a minute. Then Greg said, "Okay. Let's ask her."

Cathy, Paul's sister, listened carefully as the boys talked.

"What's the first thing we have to do?" she asked
them.

"What we need first is a rope."

"No. First, we need a ruler."

"Good ideas," said Cathy. "What's next?"

"Boards."

"A floor."

"That's great! Now we can start to make our plan for the tree house."

Cathy helped them to draw a picture of the tree house they were going to build. It looked like this.

Which photo was taken from above? Which from below? Which from the side?

They spent the afternoon climbing the big maple, and measuring. They needed to know how long to cut the pieces of wood.

Everyone worked hard. They didn't even want to stop for supper. The plan was taking shape.

The next day, Cathy came out to help. The boys found it hard at first to saw the wood and hammer in the nails. When Cathy showed them how, it became easier. Soon the floor was finished.

"Who's going to test the floor?" asked Cathy. "We'd better get some of the parents to do it. They'll want to make sure it's safe. Then we can build the rest of the tree house on it."

14 Greg quietly closed his front door. The big test was today. Walking down the street, he was thinking of the rest of the tree house, blue door and all!

▶ 1. The boys decided to get help with their problem. Was this a good decision? Why, or why not?

▶ 2. Where do you go for help when you have these problems?
   (a) A button pops off your sweater.
   (b) You are lost in a crowd.
   (c) You can't do a math question at school.
   (d) You can't do a math question in your homework.
   (e) The chain comes off your bike.
   (f) Your dog runs away from home.
   (g) Your tooth aches.
   (h) You lose your lunch.

▶ 3. (a) What do you think Greg's mother said to him before she gave him the hammer and saw?
   (b) What advice would you give the boys about these things?
   - climbing a tree
   - climbing a ladder
   - using a saw
   - using a hammer

▶ 4. When we build something or have a project, we need a *plan*.
   (a) What are some classroom projects we need a plan for?
   (b) What projects around your home must be planned?

▶ 5. Think about the plan used in your class for dismissals.
   (a) What happens first? second?
   (b) What do you do after that?

2 A Family Picnic

The Invitation

Just as the Greco family was about to sit down for supper, the phone rang.

"Hello, Maria? Is your papa there?"

"Sure, Uncle Joe." Maria held out the phone. "Papa, it's for you."

"Thanks, Maria."

From the other room, Pino could hear only a few words.

"Good. Sunday is fine...by noon...paint...picnic."

"I wonder what Papa is planning," he thought.

Mr. Greco hung up the phone and went into the kitchen. The family was waiting for him.

"Guess what! That was Uncle Joe. He wants us to go to the farm tomorrow for a picnic."

"The farm!" yelled Maria. "Whoopee!"

"There is a small catch, though. Uncle Joe has been sick. Now he needs some help to catch up with his work. The barn needs to be painted and the roof patched. Some other things have to be fixed, too." Mr. Greco

turned to his elder son. "Frank, I'll need you to help get all the tools together." Then he joined his family at the table.

Maria said, "We haven't been there for a long time. Do they still keep chickens?"

"Quiet. Grace first." Mrs. Greco bowed her head, and the family said the prayer together.

"I wonder if they have a horse yet?" Before anyone could answer Maria, Pino broke in.

"Who will be there?" he asked.

"Everybody—you'll see." Mrs. Greco began serving the vegetables. "When someone needs help, the whole family turns out. Most of your aunts and uncles will be there. So will your grandfather and grandmother. Non-

no's the best carpenter in the family. And Nonna's the
best cook."

Mr. Greco answered Maria. "No horses, as far as I know, but there are lots of chickens."

"Maria, you'll have to get ready for bed by yourself tonight," said Mrs. Greco. "We'll be leaving early tomorrow. I have a lot to do." She turned to Pino. "And you can help me prepare the salad."

Sleep didn't come to Maria for a long time. All she could think of was playing with her cousins and chasing chickens.

▶ 1. Think about a family picnic you have taken or would like to take.
   (a) Who went with you?
   (b) Where did you go?
   (c) How did you get there?
   (d) What food did you take?

▶ 2. What would be the differences between a summer picnic and a winter picnic? Think about food, clothes, and games.

▶ 3. What tools will the Grecos need to take with them?

▶ 4. Everyone is going to the farm to help. What sort of work do you share where you live? On your own paper, write sentences that finish these thoughts. Use the name of a person for each blank.
   (a) My ____ helps me by . . .
   (b) I help my ____ by . . .
   (c) My ____ helps my ____ by . . .

▶ 5. You can help people who are members of your family. You can also help other people. What is something you could do to be a good neighbour? a good friend?

Mr. and Mrs. Greco  (Grandfather and Grandmother)

They had four children: FRANK, JOE, LUCY, and TONY.

FRANK Anna   JOE Pat   John LUCY   TONY Mary

Greco   Greco   Taylor   Greco

Now the four children have families of their own.

Frank Maria Pino   Jim Helen   Mark   Doug Kim Rose

Greco   Greco   Taylor   Greco

1. *How many people are there in Grandfather and Grandmother Greco's family?*
2. *Why is one family called Taylor and not Greco?*
3. *How many cousins does Maria expect to see at the picnic?*
4. *What are the names of Uncle Tony's nephews? Who are his nieces?*
5. *Make a family tree. Your teacher will help you.*

The Trip

Mr. Greco got up very early to pack the car.

Maria slept in. She would have to hurry through her breakfast. As she was getting dressed, she heard her mother say, "Be careful with this. It's the salad. Keep it this way up. I don't want it ruined."

"Don't worry, Mama. You're talking to an expert packer," answered Frank. He was helping to take things out to the car.

At last they were ready to leave.

"Mama, did you check the windows and the stove?" called Pino from the front door.

"Yes, Pino. Close the door tight, and come on!"

They drove to the end of the block. "How much farther is it?" asked Maria.

Pino groaned. "Oh, Maria. You always ask that as soon as we get in the car. It takes an hour and a half to get to the farm."

"No, I mean how far is it?"

"About ninety kilometres," Frank told her. "Now why don't you watch out the window?"

▶ Why did Mrs. Greco check the windows and stove before Pino locked the door? What is checked in your home before it is locked up?

The time passed quickly. They were getting near the farm when they drove over a bridge. Maria pointed to the stream below. "That's where we caught the big fish with Uncle Joe last summer."

In another minute they turned off the road. This was the long lane that led into the farm. As the car came to the end, the Greco family could see cars parked all over the farmyard. There were many people standing and talking in front of the old farmhouse.

Mr. Greco stopped the car and turned off the motor.

24   Everyone scrambled out. Uncle Joe walked over to meet them. Mr. Greco punched him on the shoulder and gave him a big hug. Uncle Tony and Aunt Mary came over. They were all happy to see each other. Pino, Frank, and Maria raced over to join their cousins on the hay wagon.

The whole Greco family had come to the picnic. But first, there were things to do.

▶ When everyone arrived at the farm, they were happy to see one another. What do you like most about members of your family, or about the other people you may live with? Write one or two words that tell something about each one of them.

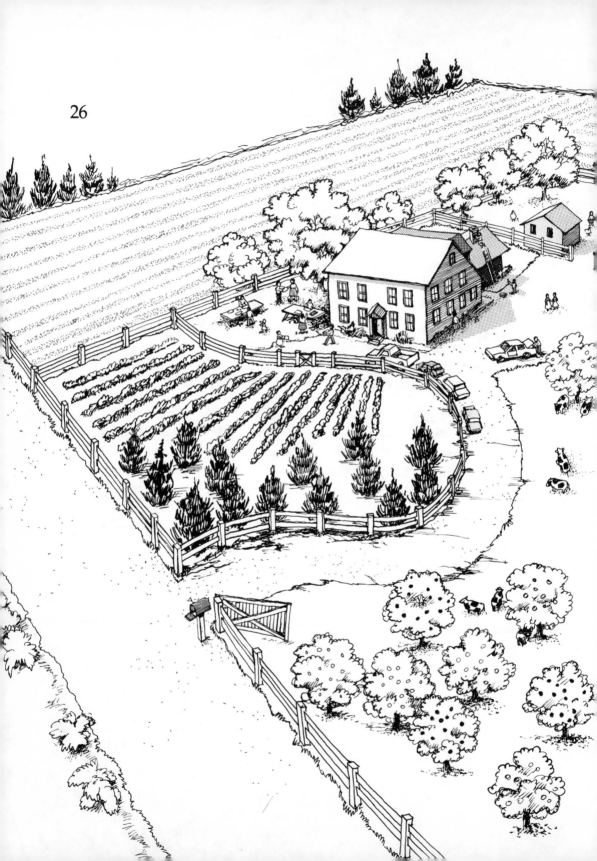

At the Farm

Look at the picture map of the farm.

▶ 1. (a) Which is taller, the farmhouse or the barn?
   (b) Which is wider, the drive shed or the chicken coop?

▶ 2. Why is there a fence around the vegetable garden?

▶ 3. Mr. Greco drove up the road from the bottom of the picture.
   (a) Which way did he turn to go up the driveway?
   (b) On which side of the driveway did he see the vegetable garden?
   (c) What did the family see to the left of the farmhouse?

▶ 4. If you could visit the farm, where would you go first? What would you do?

The Picnic

Now that the family had arrived, Uncle Joe wanted to get started. He thanked everyone for coming. Then he said,

"Let's get the work done first. After that, we'll have lots of time to visit.

"John, you said you'd look at the water pipes. The ones in the bathroom are leaking. And Tony, the bricks on the chimney are loose. The ladder is against the wall."

Then he looked at Papa. "What do you want to do?"

"Anything you like. I'm good with a hammer or a paint brush."

"Fine. The fence at the back needs a few nails. You can start there."

"I'm going with him," said Mama.

"Good idea. Four hands are better than two."

Pino and Frank went over to help their grandfather. He was already at work, fixing a broken window frame. They liked being with Nonno. He always had time to talk to his grandchildren. Perhaps today he would tell them one of their favourite stories.

Everyone worked hard all morning. Maria, too. She cleaned out the chicken coop with Mark. Finally, it was time for the picnic.

"Lunch time," Aunt Anna called. The food had been set out on tables under the trees.

It was a wonderful picnic. The food was delicious, and the air was cool in the shade of the tall maples. After lunch, some of the grown-ups went back to work. Some sat around and talked. The children played games.

It had been a perfect day. Maria was so tired that she fell asleep on the return trip. She dreamt that she was being chased home by Uncle Joe's chickens.

Which foods on the picnic table could have come from Uncle Joe's farm? (Look back at the picture of the farm for clues.) Which foods do you think came from a store?

► 1. There is a lot of work to be done around any home. Most of
the jobs can be shared. How are these jobs shared where
you live? How do you help?
(a) cooking meals
(b) cutting the grass
(c) shopping for food
(d) housecleaning
(e) ironing clothes
(f) washing and drying dishes

► 2. Does any person do more work at your home than others?
Who? Why?

► 3. Could the jobs be shared more evenly? How?

3 Runaway Red

Escape

"Come, Red. Come!"

Vera called again. Her dog was just a red streak against the green grass of the park. At the sound of her voice, Red stopped. She looked over at Vera for a moment. Then Red tossed her head. She was off again.

Vera felt like crying. She had been warned to keep Red on a leash. For one thing, Red had no sense in traffic. For another, there was a law against dogs running loose. But Red liked to run free, so Vera had let her off the leash.

1. *What are the people in this park doing?*
2. *What season of the year is it? How can you tell?*
3. *How is your park the same as this park near Vera's home? How is it different?*

Red ran up to someone lying on the grass. She stuck
her nose in the person's face, wagging her tail.

"Grab her! Catch her for me, please," Vera called. But when Red heard Vera's voice, she jumped away. First she barked at the children on the swings. Then she ran through the middle of a soccer game. She knocked over a litter basket on the other side of the park.

"Come, Red. Here, girl." Vera ran to catch her dog, but Red didn't want to come. She wanted to go! She raced up the street. Soon she was out of sight.

Vera stood with the leash in her hand. "What do I do now?" she thought.

▶ 1. Vera was told to keep Red on a leash but she let her dog run free. Now she has a problem.
   (a) What can you remember doing that led to a problem for you?
   (b) How did you feel?
   (c) Were you able to solve your problem? How?

▶ 2. How can Vera find her dog?

▶ 3. What laws are there about dogs in your community?

▶ 4. What park do you play in? What do you enjoy doing there?

The Search

The park was halfway between Vera's town house and the school. Red had headed up the mountain toward the school.

"I'll try the school first," Vera thought. "Perhaps someone will know where Red went. I can call home from there, too."

There was no sign of Red in the schoolyard. Perhaps she was hidden among the redwoods. The big trees stretched up the slope behind the school. Vera decided to look for Mr. Clark, the janitor.

"No, I haven't seen your Irish setter," said Mr. Clark. "Sure. Use the phone. Be my guest."

"Hello, Mom? Red got away from me . . . I let her off the leash. I know . . . I'm sorry. I'm at the school now. There's no sign of Red and . . . " Vera couldn't help herself. She began to cry.

Mrs. Pachuk was glad that Vera had called. She could help.

"Let's not worry too much," she said. "Red hasn't been fed today. She's never missed dinnertime yet. Start for home and keep your eyes open."

▶ 1. How could Mrs. Pachuk help?

▶ 2. Vera called home because of a family rule. What do you think the rule might be?

▶ 3. What are the rules where you live about
    (a) using the phone?
    (b) going to bed?
    (c) getting up in the morning?
    (d) coming home from school?
    (e) visiting friends?
    (f) inviting friends to your home?

▶ 1. Which is closer to Vera's home, the fire hall or the church?

▶ 2. What is a boundary? What are the boundaries of Vera's neighbourhood? What are the boundaries of your neighbourhood?

▶ 3. What is a block? How many blocks are there in Vera's neighbourhood? Are there blocks in your neighbourhood? If so, how many?

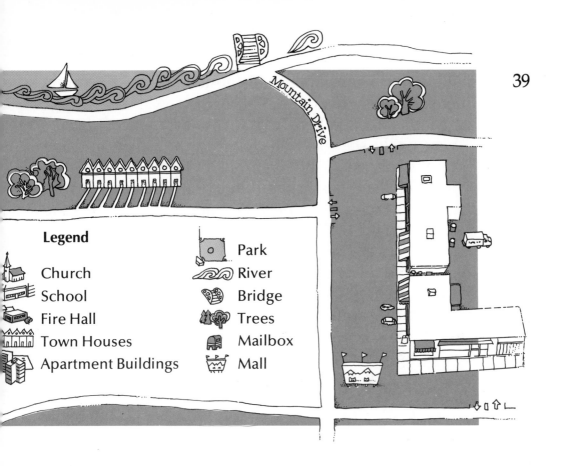

Legend

Church
School
Fire Hall
Town Houses
Apartment Buildings

Park
River
Bridge
Trees
Mailbox
Mall

On the Trail

At the corner, Vera met a letter carrier. He was scooping mail from a mailbox into a big canvas bag. He'd left the engine of his mail van running.

"Have you seen a red setter on your route?" Vera asked him.

"Almost ran one down coming up the hill. He jumped out right in front of me."

"She, not he," said Vera. "If it was Red, it was she."

"Well, I don't know about that." The letter carrier shut and locked the mailbox door. "Last I saw of her, she was making for the alley behind Mountain Mall." He threw the mailbag into his van.

"Thanks," called Vera. "Thanks a lot."

Vera could see the mall down in the valley, and the bridge that crossed the river. The block of town houses where she lived lay on the other side of the park. Vera didn't want to give up now. Perhaps if she hurried she could get to the mall and still be home by dinnertime.

Just then Vera heard the beat of a helicopter. It passed over the red tower of the old fire hall and the shiny spire of the church. She wondered if the pilot could see Red.

Vera didn't walk around the block. She cut straight through. She wouldn't do that just anywhere, but here it was all right. She knew the people—besides, this was an emergency. The next block was all apartments. She cut through the parking lot between them.

"Hold everything, Red," she thought to herself. "I'm on my way."

▶ 1. Going onto private property without permission is called trespassing. Was Vera trespassing? Explain what you think.

▶ 2. What was the letter carrier doing? How was he helping in Vera's neighbourhood?

▶ 3. What other helpers are there in your neighbourhood? Keep a record for a week of all the helpers you see in that time and what you see them doing.

▶ 4. Look again at the map of Vera's neighbourhood. Use your finger to trace Vera's route from her home to the park, to the school, to Mountain Mall.

1. *What kinds of homes do people live in, in Vera's neighbourhood?*
2. *What kinds of homes do people in your neighbourhood live in?*
3. *What other kinds of buildings do you see in the photographs?*

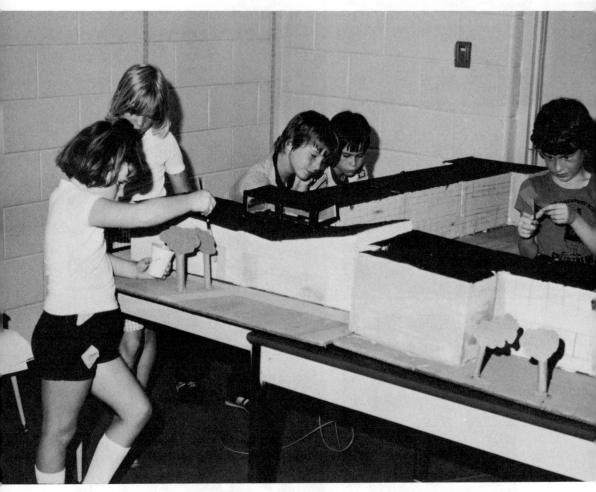

What are these children doing? What materials are they using? What plans do you think they made before they started?

Make plans for a model of your neighbourhood. What details are you going to include in your model? Decide what materials you will need.

Vera was out of breath when she reached the mall. She had run all the way. On her way down, she had been thinking. If Red were in the alley, she'd take off as soon as she saw Vera coming.

"I'm going to need some help." Vera thought of Mr. Kotka at the variety store. He was a friend. Madame Lu at the beauty salon liked Red. Vera knew they would help if they could. But they were busy people, and the mall was crowded that afternoon.

Then Vera noticed the group of people at the variety store window. One of them was a friend. She broke into a run.

"Hey, Bill! Come and help me—please! Red got away from me and I think she's behind the mall." Vera gave Bill no time to answer. She caught his arm and dragged him away from the window.

"Okay, okay, I'll help. Hey, there's a picture of you in the window! All right, I'm coming. What do you want me to do?"

"I'm going around this end of the mall. You go around the other end. If you see Red, grab her!" Vera gave Bill a push and she started off in the other direction.

Red was in the alley. She had turned over two garbage cans behind the restaurant. She was easy to catch, as she didn't want to leave the garbage.

"Whew! What a smell." Bill held his nose.

"That's Red," said Vera. "She's rolled in something."

"Let's get out of here."

"I can't leave this mess, Bill. Red did it, but it's really

44 my fault. Will you hold her for me? I'll tidy this up."

It didn't take long. Afterwards, Bill wanted to show Vera the picture display at the variety store.

"The window's full of pictures of the Mountain Mall Dog Show. There's one of you and Red."

"Really? She won first prize," said Vera proudly. "But I can't look now. I have to get home. Besides, she smells too much!"

They both looked down at Red. She certainly didn't look like a prize-winner.

▶ 1. Look back at the map and pictures of Vera's neighbourhood.
   (a) How is Vera's neighbourhood very different from yours?
   (b) How is it very much the same?

▶ 2. What do you like most about your neighbourhood?

▶ 3. What is there for people to do in your neighbourhood? List all the activities you can think of on a chart like this.

Children	Grown-ups	Everybody

Belonging to a Community

4 Emergency!

At the Crosswalk

It was a cold, wet day. The rain lay in puddles all over the street. All of a sudden, a bell rang. Children in bright plastic raincoats spilled into the yard. School was out.

An umbrella, down the street, looked like a shiny black mushroom with four legs.

Christie and Karl Devin were underneath the umbrella. They were on their way home.

Karl pulled the umbrella down close to their heads. All Christie could see was the patch of sidewalk under her feet. She kept quiet until they reached the corner. Then she stepped out of the shelter of the umbrella.

"You can have it," Christie said to Karl. "I can't see anything under that thing."

They were standing at the curb. Mr. Laporte, the crossing guard, was on the other side of the busy street. He had just taken a group of children across.

"Wait right there. I'll come over for you," called Mr. Laporte. That was one of his rules. Everyone knew they had to wait for him. Sometimes, though, people would forget the rules, or break them.

Mr. Laporte took no chances. He was polite but firm. There had never been an accident on his crosswalk while he was on duty. "Safety first" was his motto.

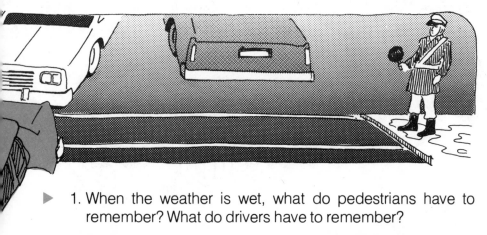

▶ 1. When the weather is wet, what do pedestrians have to remember? What do drivers have to remember?

▶ 2. What sort of safety rules do you think Mr. Laporte would make for his crosswalk?

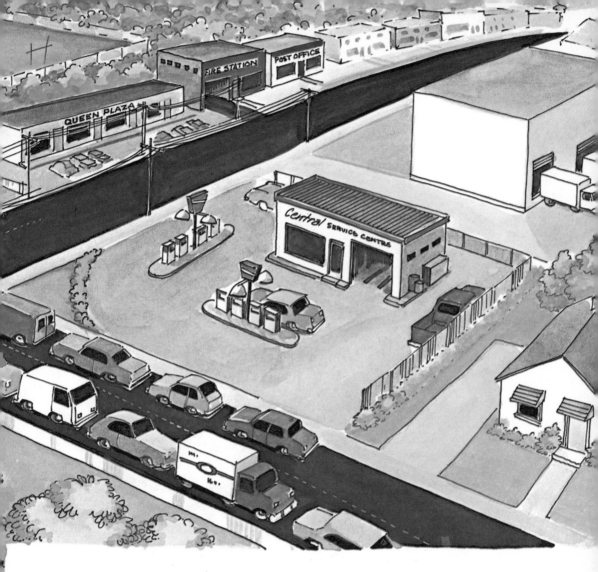

1. What is the largest building in the neighbourhood? What is the smallest?

2. In which buildings do people live? In which buildings do they work?

3. Which building is nearer to the shopping plaza, the school or the garage?

4. Which house is closest to the crosswalk?

5. Where in the neighbourhood do people play games? What games can they play?

Who are the people on this page? In what way are their jobs the same?

How can you tell that Mr. Laporte is a crossing guard? What is he wearing? What is he carrying?

The Accident

Mr. Laporte watched the road for a break in the traffic. He didn't see the girl on the bicycle riding on the sidewalk. She didn't stop. She rode past the children into the road.

Then everything seemed to happen at once. There was a scream and a screech of brakes. A car skidded over the wet road. Christie jumped, but Karl seemed rooted to the spot. The car slid onto the sidewalk. It smashed into a hydro pole.

Christie heard the sound of breaking glass. She saw the hydro pole snap in the middle. A few wires held it up.

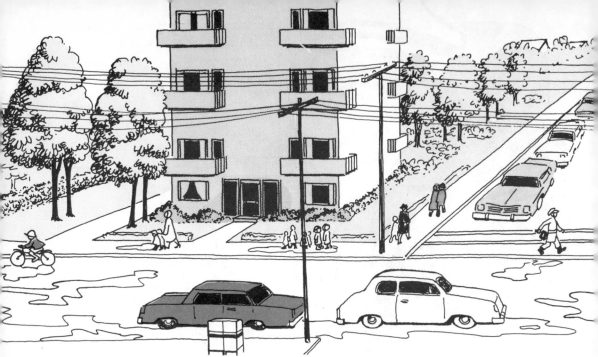

At first there was silence. Then Mr. Laporte ran up to Christie.

"Where's Karl?" he asked. "What happened to him?"

"There he is on the sidewalk." Christie pointed. Karl was just sitting up. He was rubbing his head and crying. "The car bounced back off the pole and knocked him down. I think he hit his head on the sidewalk," Christie said.

"Go over and stay with him for a minute," said Mr. Laporte. "I want to see if the driver of the car is hurt."

There was a woman with Karl when Christie reached him.

"Are you all right, Karl?" Christie asked.

Karl shook his head. "Where...where's my umbrella?" he sobbed.

"Never mind your umbrella," the woman said. "You can borrow mine. I've phoned for the police and an ambulance. We'll have you fixed up in no time."

There was no sign of the girl on the bicycle. She had vanished.

▶ 1. How do you think Christie felt when she saw Karl rubbing his head and crying?

▶ 2. Who do you think was the woman with Karl?

▶ 3. What would you do first if you saw an accident like this? Would you call the police, Karl's parents, or an ambulance? Why?

▶ 4. What safety rules do you remember when you are
    (a) playing on the street?
    (b) riding your bicycle?
    (c) crossing the road?
    (d) riding on the school bus?
    (e) playing in the schoolyard?

The Police Officer

Christie heard the siren first. It grew louder and louder. Then she saw the police car. It stopped beside them. The red lights were flashing.

The police officer went over to Karl.

"Is he hurt?" she asked the woman.

"Just bruised and scared, I think."

"Did you see what happened?"

"No, I was in the house."

"I did. I did. I was here all the time." Christie was jumping up and down with all the excitement. She could hear more sirens now.

"Don't go away, then, please. I'd like to speak with you later." The officer went back to her car. She returned with a blanket. She tucked it around Karl's shoulders. Karl was still shaking, but he had stopped crying.

"I'll be right back," said the officer.

She walked over to the wrecked car. The driver was inside. Mr. Laporte had been helping him. She asked Mr. Laporte to move the people back. He moved them away from the accident—away from the fallen wires.

The radio in the cruiser crackled. The officer picked up the handset. She was ready to make her report.

▶ 1. How did the people at the scene of the accident help one another?

▶ 2. What other helpers are needed? What will they do at the scene of the accident?

▶ 3. Why did the officer want the crowd moved back? What might happen?

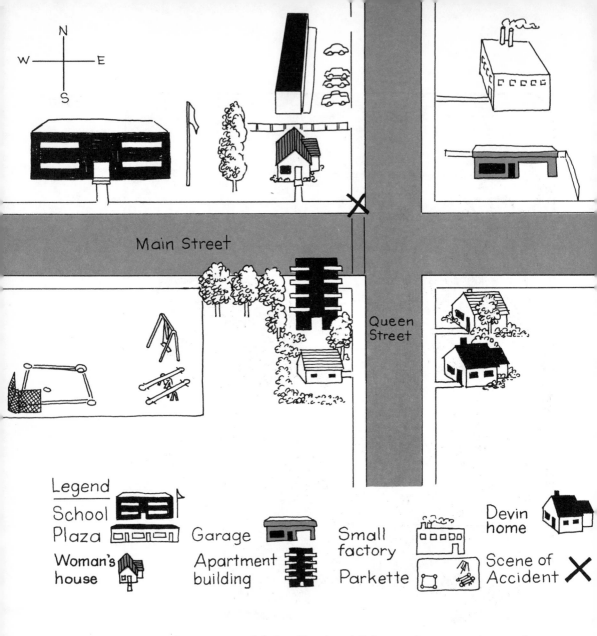

- ► 1. What route did the Devin children take to go home from school?
- ► 2. How did they get to the shopping plaza from their home?
- ► 3. Is the school to the left or right of the crosswalk?
- ► 4. What buildings are close to the scene of the accident?

The ambulance was next to arrive. Its siren faded out. Two men pulled out a stretcher bed.

"Can you stand up, son?" one of them asked Karl. He helped Karl to his feet.

"He doesn't need the stretcher," the other man said. "Help him to the ambulance. We'd better take him to Eastern Hospital, just in case. I'll check the driver in the car."

They had to lift the driver out of his car. They needed the stretcher for him. His leg had been hurt.

The ambulance was ready to go.

"So long, Karl."

"See you, Christie." Karl looked happier now. He didn't mind riding in the ambulance. He hoped the driver would use the siren.

58   Christie was glad to stay. So much was happening at the crosswalk.

As the ambulance left, a hydro truck arrived. It had a sign on it in big letters: EMERGENCY VEHICLE. The hydro workers started to move the wires that lay on the road. They didn't waste any time. Christie moved closer to watch. The police officer called to her.

"Hey, young lady. Stay close to me. I need you here."

Two more trucks rolled up to the intersection. More people got out.

"Now what?" said Christie to the officer.

"That's the telephone company's truck and the other's a tow truck."

"Is that all, then?"

"No. There's one more to come—a fire engine. The

gas from the car has to be hosed off the sidewalk." The officer smiled at Christie. "Now, I'll drive you home, and we'll tell your parents what's happened."

▶ 1. Which vehicle got to the accident
  (a) first?   (d) fourth?
  (b) second?   (e) fifth?
  (c) third?   (f) sixth?

▶ 2. Everyone had a job to do. In what order do you think each job should be done?

▶ 3. Why is it important for emergency cars and trucks to get to an accident quickly?

▶ 4. The girl on the bicycle who caused the accident knew what had happened. What would she be thinking? How do you think she feels?

Soon everything was back to normal in the Devin house.

The phone rang. "It's for you, Mom," said Karl. "It's Mrs. Kirk."

Mrs. Devin listened to Mrs. Kirk for a long time. Then she spoke. "A petition is a great idea! I agree with you. We do need traffic lights at that corner.

"No. Nobody has been killed yet. But there have been six accidents there this year.

"The City Council won't do anything unless we ask. A petition is the first step. Thanks for calling, Pam. Good-bye." Mrs. Devin hung up.

"What's a petition, Mom?" asked Christie.

"Well, we are going to write a letter to the mayor. It will tell him about the problems at Queen and Main. All of the people who want a set of lights there will sign it. The letter will be our petition."

What do you think he did?

November 21

The Mayor
City Hall

We want traffic lights at Main and
Queen, please. The traffic on Main
is very heavy. There is an accident
at the crosswalk almost every month.
We are afraid for our children. We
are afraid for ourselves.

George and Freda Naumoff

Mike Day   Pam Kirk

Vi Denin   Paul Auchin

Dippy Devin   Eva Starchuk

Marry Day   Mark Starchuk
Alan Cotton   Fred Kirk

Mr. and Mrs. Otto Kubalasa

5 The Santa Claus Parade

Before the Parade

On the first Saturday in December, Santa comes to town. Everyone is happy to see him. There is a big parade. Everyone in it dresses up. Many other people come out to watch the parade and greet Santa Claus.

The Furness family likes to take part in the parade.
Mrs. Furness always helps to decorate a float. This year her float is called "The Bookworm".

Jane Furness is eight years old. She belongs to the Majorettes Club. This will be the second time she has marched in the parade. She has a new costume to wear.

Wayne, her older brother, is in the Air Cadets. He will be marching with the other cadets in the parade. He has to make sure that his boots and buttons are shined.

Their father has a secret. He too will be in the parade, but he won't tell what he will be doing. He says only that he will be there.

The week before the parade, there is a story about it in the newspaper.

SANTA CLAUS PARADE
SATURDAY

Santa is coming to town next Saturday, December 4. The parade will leave the plaza at 1:00 p.m. It will finish at the arena. Santa will be welcomed by a record number of bands, floats, and clowns.

The weather forecast is for a sunny, cold parade day.

On the weekend before the parade, many people are busy. Costumes have to be finished. Floats have to be painted and polished.

Solving Problems

For many weeks a group of people has been meeting. They talk about the parade. They want to make sure that nothing goes wrong.

"What will we do if it snows?"

"What will we do if Santa is sick that day?"

"How will we stop the crowds from getting on the road and into the parade?"

"What if someone gets hurt?"

What other problems do you think the planners talked about?

The Day of the Parade

Saturday finally arrives. There is great excitement in town. The Furness family is up bright and early.

After breakfast Mrs. Furness leaves the house. She has a few things to finish on the Bookworm.

Mr. Furness drives Jane to the high school. The majorettes are meeting there. He drops Wayne off at the park. The air cadets are there.

Just as she gets out of the car, Jane looks at her father. "You still haven't said what you are going to do in the parade. Please tell us," she says.

Her father replies with a twinkle in his eye.

"You'll see me. Have a good time in the parade! 'Bye for now."

66 ▶ 1. Locate the following places on the map.
   (a) plaza   (d) church
   (b) police station (e) fire station
   (c) shops   (f) arena

▶ 2. What building is across from the fire station?

▶ 3. What is next to the fire station?

▶ 4. Which building is smaller, the gas station or the hotel?

▶ 5. What directions would you have to give to explain the route of the Santa Claus parade?

Legend Route of parade ● ● ● ●

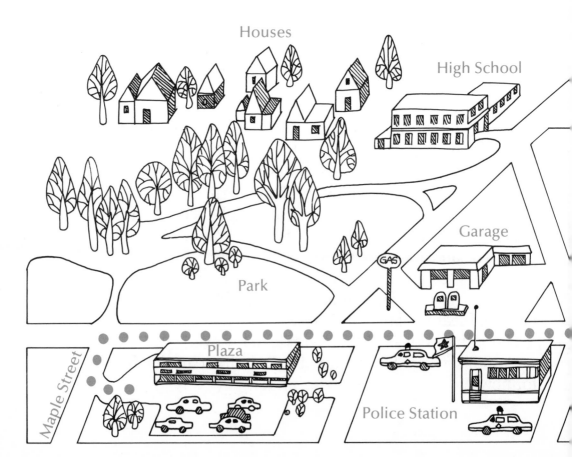

Arena

Houses

67

School

River Street

Swimming Pool

Apartments

Post Office

POST OFFICE

Ritz

Hotel

Church Street

Fire Station

King Street

Church

Mill Street

Main Street

Shops

Many people have jobs to do in the parade. They all work together.

Police officers are very busy during a parade. They make sure that everyone is safe. What problems might they expect in this parade?

The person who is in charge of the parade is called the parade marshal. The marshal's place is at the beginning of the route. People in the parade are told when to start. There are other marshals along the route. How do you think they talk to one another? What problems might they have?

A Radio Conversation

PARADE MARSHAL: Pat, this is Don. How does the parade look from the church? Over.

ROUTE MARSHAL: Hi, Don. Everything is going fine. Five floats have gone by. They are all moving well. Hold it! The old fire truck has just stopped. Over.

PARADE MARSHAL: Oh, no! I was afraid that might happen. Over.

ROUTE MARSHAL: You can relax now, Don. The driver just got it going again. Over.

PARADE MARSHAL: Thanks, Pat. I'll talk to you again later. Over and out.

70

Mrs. Jones is driving a tractor in the parade. It is pulling the Cinderella float. What would happen if she drove too fast?

Sonya Wilson belongs to the St. John Ambulance Corps. When a lot of people gather in public, Sonya and other members stand by, ready to help. What kind of help can Sonya give? Who might need her help?

Jane marches by in her bright new costume. She twirls her baton. She marches in time to the beat of the drums. How would you feel if you were Jane?

Wayne looks smart in his uniform. Most of the cadets are in step. They swing their arms briskly. Try to march in step with one of your friends. What did you have to do to keep in step?

Santa always rides on the very last float. His deep laugh can be heard above the jingle of the sleigh bells. Ho! Ho! Ho! Ho!

After Santa's sleigh has gone by, the crowd starts to go home. What a great parade! The Christmas music and Santa's laugh still ring in their ears. The parade is over for another year. The Christmas holidays will soon begin.

After the Parade

By late afternoon, all members of the Furness family are home. Their faces are still red from the cold air. The children are tired from all the marching. Hot chocolate and doughnuts help to warm them up.

As they sip their drinks, Jane suddenly looks over at her father.

"I thought you told us you were going to be in the parade. I didn't see you. Neither did Wayne."

"Are you sure you didn't see me?" asks Mr. Furness. "I was there. I saw you!" He laughs. "Ho! Ho! Ho! Ho!"

Look at the pictures of the parade. Can you find Mr. Furness? Have you guessed who he is?

▶ 1. Which project would take more planning, a tree house or a parade? Why?

▶ 2. How can an event such as a parade help people in a community get to know each other?

▶ 3. What other events can you think of, in which people in a community must work together?

▶ 4. Tell about an activity of your own that you share with others in your community. What do you do? What do the other people do?

There is a prize for the best float in the parade. Which of these floats do you think should win the prize? Why?

6 The Library That Shrank

In the middle of town stands an old grey building. The year *1877* is carved above the door.

At first, the building was a church. Then a bigger church was built. The little stone building was given to the people of the town. It is now the town library.

Public Library

Name . . . .

Address . . . .

Telephone . . . .

Signature . . . .

Date . . . .

▶ 1. Why do towns have libraries?

▶ 2. What services do libraries provide?

▶ 3. Who uses the library?

▶ 4. Who pays for it?

What Do People Think about the Old Library?

Many people visit the library. It is a busy place. It attracts people of all ages. What do the people think of their town's library?

"I love to read, and this is such a good library. It has many good books. The library was one of the reasons why we moved to this town. Some places don't have a library. The only problem is that everything is so crowded. We need a larger library."

Mrs. Collins.

Mr. Hill.

"I never use the library. I like to watch sports and TV. I hear that some people want a new library. Why should I have to pay for a new one when I don't use the one we have? What this town really needs is a new hockey arena."

Wyn.

"The lady who looks after the children's section is really nice. She helps me to choose books I like. And that's not all. Last winter Jim and I went to the library every Saturday morning. Mrs. Hodgson taught us crafts. It was fun. Next year we hope to have a science club—if there's room. Our section is in the basement. There isn't much space to do things there."

Mrs. Stubbs.

"A town library is important. So many different groups can use it. But if we build a new library, taxes will go up. I wonder what other people think about the idea."

Adult section of the library.

Children's section.

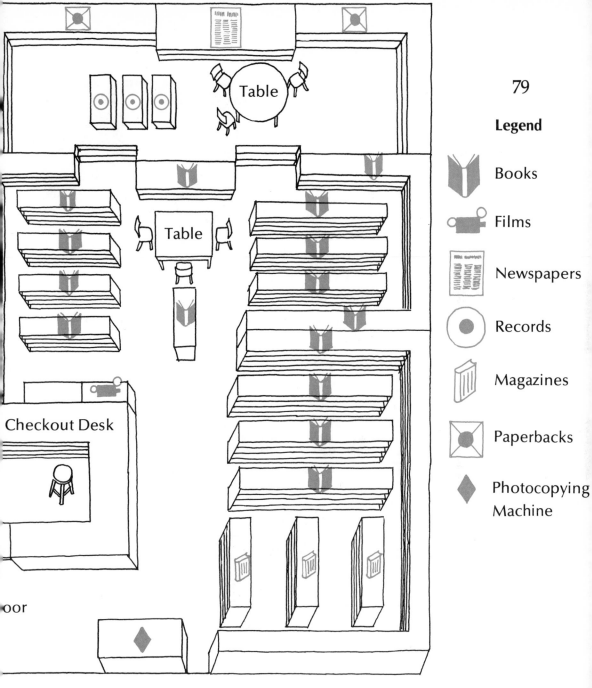

Legend

Books

Films

Newspapers

Records

Magazines

Paperbacks

Photocopying Machine

Table

Table

Checkout Desk

oor

▶ 1. What part of the library is most crowded?

▶ 2. What takes more space, books or records?

▶ 3. Where do people sit to read magazines?

80 "I've been here ever since the library first opened. Many things have changed since then. At first the old building was too big. We didn't have enough books to fill the shelves. Then the town started to grow. As more people came to live here, we had to buy more

Mr. Engels, librarian.

books. We added new services. Look at the plan of the library. There just isn't room for anything else. We've run out of space.

"I've just made up a graph. Perhaps you'd like to see it. It shows what services people use each day between three and four o'clock."

Tuesday	📖 📖 ⊙ 📖 📖 📑 📖 ◆◆
Wednesday	⊙ ⊙ ⊙ ⊠ ⊠ 📚📚📖
Thursday	📑◆📖📖📖⊙
Friday	📚📚📚📖📖📖📖📖
Saturday	◆ 📽 ⊙ ⊙ 📑📑⊠⊠⊠◆📖

▶ 1. Make a bar graph to show how much each service was used.

▶ 2. Which was used the most?

▶ 3. Which was used the least?

▶ 4. Which services would you use?

1. Draw a plan of your library, with a legend.

2. Make a pictograph of the services people use.

3. Talk to the librarian. Who uses the library the most? What problems are there?

Community Action

Several people said that the old library was too small. A bigger building was needed.

Not everyone agreed with this view. Many didn't want a new library. They thought the old one was good enough. Perhaps the town needed other things more.

People do not always agree on what is best for their community. A good community listens to all points of view. Everyone has the right to express opinions.

Mrs. Collins wondered how many people felt the way she did. She phoned her friend, Mrs. Stenner.

MRS. COLLINS: Hello, Dee.

MRS. STENNER: Janet, how are you?

MRS. COLLINS: I've just come back from the library, and I'm fed up. It's so crowded there!

MRS. STENNER: I feel the same way. There aren't enough book shelves. Or chairs and tables, for reading.

MRS. COLLINS: Don't you think we need a new library?

MRS. STENNER: Yes, I do. That's the answer. I wonder who would help us to campaign for a new library.

This was how the library project began.

Mrs. Collins and Mrs. Stenner had a meeting with everyone who wanted to help. Twenty people came. They all wanted a new library. They decided to call themselves Citizens for a New Library. Now they could begin to make plans.

A new library would cost a lot of money. Who would pay for it? The town couldn't afford to build a library for only twenty people. The group would have to prove that a new library was needed, and that most people would use it. Then the town council would be asked to listen to their request.

How could they tell all the people in town about the idea?

GETTING THE MESSAGE ACROSS

Messages are sent around your school in many different ways.

1. How does your principal get a message to you? to your teacher? to your home?

2. How do you give information to your teacher?

3. How would you send a message to a friend in another class?

A community is much larger than a school. There are more people to contact.

▶ 1. How do you think Mrs. Collins and Mrs. Stenner let people know they were going to have a meeting?

▶ 2. (a) In what different ways could the Citizens for a New Library tell others about their project?

(b) What would be the fastest way? the slowest? the best?

After thinking about it and talking it over, this is what the Citizens did.

Wrote Letters
Some people in the group were good writers. They each wrote a letter to the local newspaper. What do you think they said? How would they know what other people thought of their ideas? Where else could they send letters?

The Editor,
The Weekly News,
723 Main St.,
Foxtown,
Q3A 2B6

Visited Homes
Every member of the Citizens for a New Library agreed to visit at least ten homes. Why did they decide to visit and talk to people? What would the visitor say when someone came to the door? What could the visitor say if someone didn't like the idea? What would you say if you were asked to be a visitor?

Soon the whole town knew about the campaign for a new library. The Citizens decided it was time to have a public meeting. Anyone could come and speak. Posters went up in store windows. They showed the time and place of the meeting.

So many people came that all the seats were taken. People who were late had to stand at the back. Everyone listened to Mrs. Collins. "We have to meet in the school," she said, "because there isn't room in the library." She asked the people for their opinions.

The Citizens for a New Library found out what everyone thought. Some people disagreed, but most wanted a new library.

Before the people left, most of them signed a petition. Mrs. Collins told them that she and her group would take it to the town council. More than five hundred people signed their names.

> PETITION
>
> To   The Town Council
>
> From   The Citizens for a New Library
>
> All the people who have signed their names below want you to build a new library.

Meeting with the Town Council

The mayor and council met Mrs. Collins and her group as soon as they could. They had been elected to look after the town. They were pleased to listen. What people told them helped them decide what was best for the town.

Mrs. Collins told them why her group had been formed and what the Citizens had done. She gave facts about the need for more library space. Then she gave them the petition. This proved to the council that most people wanted a new library.

Mayor Pomeroy thanked her. After a long discussion the council agreed to find out how much a new library would cost. And at its next meeting, the council voted 9-3 in favour of a new library.

Mrs. Collins' dream would come true.

▶ What kinds of facts might Mrs. Collins have used to prove that more space was needed? Where would she get this information?

Community Action

You have learned how people can get things done in a community. What needs changing in your community? Choose a project.

How will you tell others about your project? Each person in your class can help. Here are some ideas.

RADIO BROADCAST
Pretend you are a radio newscaster. Tell all about the project.

WRITE A LETTER
Whom do you want to tell about the project? Write them a short letter. Give all the facts.

TELEPHONE
Use the telephone to contact people. What will you say?

PAINT A POSTER
Invite everyone to attend a public meeting. What should you put on the poster?

PUT ON A PLAY
Write a short play about the project. Who will be in the play? What will they say? Put on the play for the rest of your class.

All Around Town

7 Saturday at the Arena

Getting Together

Bill yanked his hockey equipment out of the closet. His team sweater was missing.

"Mom! Where's my hockey sweater?"

"In the dryer," Mrs. Krupp answered. "What's the hurry? It's only 9:25."

"*Only* 9:25! I'm in trouble!"

Mrs. Drexel, Fred's mother, was picking Bill up in five

minutes. Bill and Fred had to be at the arena half an hour before their 10:30 a.m. game. The coach wanted to talk to the team.

Bill pulled on his sweater. He was proud of the blue and black sweater with *Wolves* printed on the crest. But it was going to take more than smart-looking sweaters to beat the Falcons. They were the top team in the league.

A car horn sounded.

"'Bye," called Bill as he rushed out of the house. He quickly did up his coat. The temperature was −7°C.

In the car, Fred told him they were going to pick up two other players, Ted and Sherri. Ted played defence and Sherri was the goaltender for the Wolves. Bill and Fred were forwards.

Mrs. Drexel had to stop at the gas station first. Then they were on their way again. After two more stops to pick up Ted and Sherri, they pulled into the arena's parking lot.

"Let's go!" shouted Fred. The four children rushed for the entrance.

"You forgot something." Mrs. Drexel's voice stopped them, and they turned back to the car.

"What?" asked Fred. "I've got everything."

Bill checked his bag. "Me too. What did we forget?"

"You forgot to say thank you," said Mrs. Drexel. "And if you want a ride home, meet me here at noon. I'm going up to the lounge to help set up the arts and crafts show." As she spoke, she opened the trunk of the car. She pulled out two macramé owls she had made and shook them free.

"Can we help?" asked Sherri.

"No, thanks. I can manage."

"Thanks for the ride, Mrs. Drexel." There was a chorus of thank-you's. Then the children were off in a flurry of snow.

As soon as they stepped inside the arena, they smelled smoke!

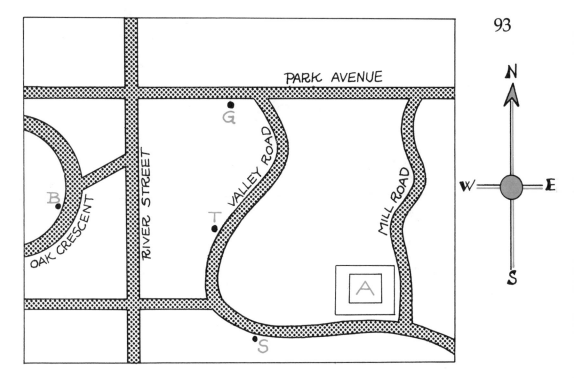

Legend

B Bill's House

T Ted's Apartment

S Sherri's House

G Gas Station

A Arena

1. *What is the difference between a street and a crescent? Is your home on a street, crescent, avenue, or road? If not, what is it on?*
2. *Who lives closest to the arena, Sherri, Bill, or Ted? Who lives farthest away?*
3. *Where did Mrs. Drexel go after she left Bill's house? With your finger, trace her route from Bill's house to the arena.*
4. *In what direction is the arena from Sherri's house? In what direction is it from Park Avenue?*

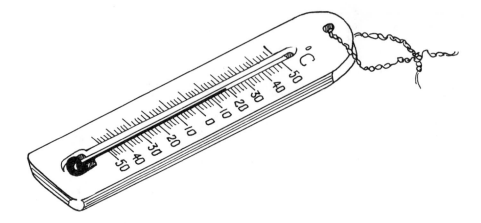

▶ 1. Draw four thermometers. Colour each thermometer to show the temperature
   (a) when Bill stepped outside,
   (b) when you left home this morning,
   (c) inside your classroom now,
   (d) outside at recess.

▶ 2. This chart shows what Bill was doing at different times on Saturday.
   9:25 a.m.   Bill finds his sweater.
   9:30 a.m.   Mrs. Drexel picks up Bill in her car.
   10:00 a.m.   Bill meets his coach.
   10:30 a.m.   The Wolves play the Falcons.
   Now make a chart of what *you* were doing at different times last Saturday. Start with the time you got out of bed.

▶ 3. Mrs. Drexel and Mrs. Krupp took turns driving the children to the arena. The children seemed to expect it.
   (a) Why didn't the children walk?
   (b) In what other ways might the children depend on their families to help them play hockey?
   (c) What special things does your family do for you?

▶ 4. What people do you know who give time to help others in the community?

Teamwork

The lobby was full of boys and girls wearing skates. They were lining up to go outside. Suddenly, the loudspeaker crackled. Everyone stopped talking to listen.

"This is the arena manager speaking. I want to thank you all for your co-operation. The small fire in the equipment room is now under control. Members of the skating school can go back on the ice."

"Let's go." Ted led the way downstairs to the change room. Jim Leach, their coach, was waiting for them.

"Hurry it up, everyone. We have a lot to talk about before we go on the ice."

Just then the door opened. Mr. Trench, the arena manager, walked in. He looked worried.

"Jim, I wonder if you and your team can help me out. The machine that floods the ice was damaged in the fire. We won't be able to use it today. I need a crew to clean and flood the ice after every game."

Jim looked around at his team. Most of them nodded. "Leave it to us," he said.

"Thanks, I knew I could depend on you. A lot of groups have rented ice time, and I hate to let anyone down. Thank you, Wolves. Joe, the machine operator, will tell you what to do." Mr. Trench waved his hand and closed the door behind him.

▶ 1. (a) What groups use the arena where Bill plays hockey?
   (b) What groups use the arena nearest you? Make a picture and label it, or write a sentence about what each group does.

▶ 2. (a) Everyone belongs to groups—at home, at school, at work, at play. What groups do you belong to? Name as many as you can think of.
   (b) In the groups you belong to, who leads when it comes to
      • getting dinner ready?
      • doing bus or safety patrol?
      • planning a party for your teacher?
      • deciding where to go on a holiday?
      • earning money?
      • playing a game in the park?
      • buying clothes?
      • leading a school assembly?
      • putting out a fire?

What people are needed in an arena to make sure the activities run smoothly? What does each person do?

Planning Ahead

Last year the Wolves' first coach had moved away. One of the players asked her older brother Jim to coach the team. He was a good hockey player himself. Coaching took a lot of Jim's time, but he had never let the team down.

Jim called the players around him. "They'll be booking the ice for wedding receptions next," he said jokingly. "There's no ice time for us next Saturday. We have to play at the Pinehill Arena at six in the morning." Everybody groaned. "It's a half-hour drive from here. This map will show you how to get there. We'll meet outside my house at five."

Jim passed out copies of the map. Then he asked, "Who can drive for us? We'll need at least three cars."

"I'm sure my mom will drive," said Mary Kemp, as she tied the laces of her skates.

"My dad will, too," said another voice.

"It's my mom's turn to drive four of us next week," Bill said. "But I'll check with her."

"That should do it, then," said Jim. He looked at the clock over the door. It was almost 10:30. "We'd better move, but there's one more thing." He blocked the door so nobody could get out.

"Did anyone see the poster in the lobby?" Nobody had. The lobby had been too crowded. "There's a poster advertising a Winter Carnival. It's to raise money for ice

time and equipment. The skating school is coming in with us, but we need some more good skaters for the Ice Show. Can I count on all of you?"

"Sure."

"Sounds great."

Jim stepped away from the door. "Okay. I'll tell you more about it next week. Remember to check with Joe about cleaning the ice."

▶ 1. (a) What would have happened next Saturday if Jim had not planned for ice time at Pinehill Arena?
   (b) Do you ever have to make plans ahead of time when people are counting on you? When?

▶ 2. Make a graph like the sample here. Show what games are played by the children in your class, and the number of children who play each one. Which game is the most popular?

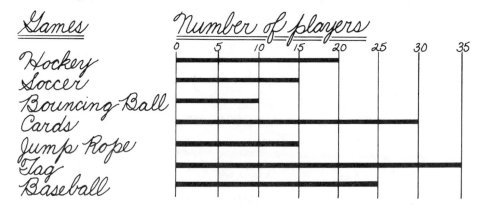

Games

Hockey
Soccer
Bouncing Ball
Cards
Jump Rope
Tag
Baseball

Number of players

0   5   10   15   20   25   30   35

▶ 3. Where is your nearest arena? Pretend you are a coach. You have called a team meeting at your house before a game. Make a map to show your team how to go from your house to the arena.

The game with the Falcons was a good one, although the Wolves lost, 6-4. Then nearly everyone disappeared. Bill, Fred, Sherri, and Ted were left to help Joe on the ice.

Fred went to find his mother. "I'll tell her we won't be going home until later."

"Tell her we'll have lunch at the snack bar," called Bill. "And the rest of us can phone home from there."

All afternoon they worked with Joe. They had to scrape the ice after every game and then flood the surface with a hose. Two girls from the skating school joined them, so Joe had all the help he needed.

Mr. Trench was pleased. "You've done me a real favour," he said to all the helpers. "Is there anything that I can do for you?"

▶ 1. What might Mr. Trench do for the boys and girls, in return for their help?

▶ 2. (a) In your neighbourhood, how do players and spectators act when their team loses?
   (b) What is "a good sport"?
   (c) Are most people good sports, or not? Explain what you think.

▶ 3. Which of the Wolves are most likely to help with the Winter Carnival? Why do you think so?

▶ 4. When the game was over, all but four Wolves failed to stay to help Joe. How would you feel if
   (a) you were one who stayed?
   (b) you were one who didn't stay?

8 Welcome to Canada

Take-off

The long red and white jet roared up into the sky. It had just taken off from the airport at Kingston, Jamaica. Soon the island of Jamaica was just a tiny dot in the ocean.

"Good morning. This is Captain Bell speaking, on Flight 712. We will be landing in Toronto in four and a half hours. The temperature there is minus twelve degrees Celsius, with snow expected. I hope you will enjoy your trip."

Troy Campbell and his mother were among the 210 passengers on the plane. Troy was excited. He had never flown before. In fact, this was the first time he had left his island home. This was a very special day for Troy and his mother. They were going to join Mrs. Campbell's brother Ken and live in Canada.

▶ 1. Troy had left his friends behind in Jamaica. How would you feel if you had to leave your home and your friends?

▶ 2. Troy will be going to a Canadian school. How should we treat newcomers? What can we do to make a new pupil feel welcome?

▶ 3. The temperature in Toronto is −12°C. What clothes will Troy need to wear?

On Board Flight 712

The first Canadian Troy had met was the flight attendant on the plane. He had smiled at Troy and his mother as they looked for their seats. Perhaps he could tell that they were a little bit scared.

Troy looked through the window beside his seat. The sky was bright and clear. He could see only water below. Soon he began to feel hungry. He hadn't eaten since very early that morning. Some strange, new smells were coming from the galley. Lunch was being served.

The flight attendant brought trays of food to Troy and Mrs. Campbell. There were small dishes on the trays. Troy wasn't sure he would like this food. He tried the small steak. It was tasty. But it wasn't as good as the spicy chicken and rice his mother often cooked.

After lunch, the attendant spoke to Troy. He had a surprise for him. Would Troy like to meet the captain and his crew? Troy's eyes lit up. He sure would!

Troy walked quickly to the front of the plane. Captain
Bell was expecting him. There were two other crew members in the cockpit. One of them was eating her lunch. The other was wearing headphones. Captain Bell explained to Troy what some of the controls were for. Troy had never seen so many buttons and dials in his life. What a lot pilots had to know to fly a plane! Troy was no longer nervous. He and his mother were safe with the crew of Flight 712.

Touch-down

Late in the afternoon, the big jet started down. The airport was just a few minutes ahead. Troy's ears began to pop. His mother told him to swallow a few times. He felt better after that. Suddenly, he could see some rooftops through the window. And snow—the first he had ever seen! He would have a lot of things to ask his uncle about Canada.

Soon the long runway came into sight. With a slight bump and a sharp squeal of tires, the plane touched down. Flight 712 had landed.

"Welcome to Canada," said the flight attendant.

These were the words that Troy and his mother had been waiting for. Their long trip was nearly over. They had reached their new country.

▶ 1. Who would look after a passenger who was sick or hurt on the plane? What kind of training would be needed for this job?

▶ 2. How does a plane keep in touch with an airport? Which member of an air crew has this job?

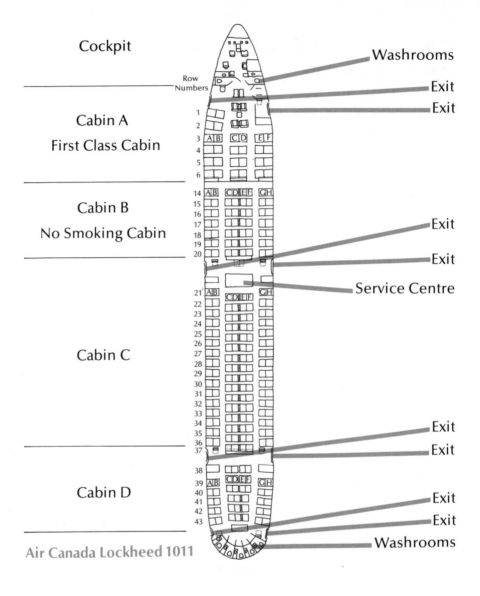

Cockpit

Washrooms

Exit

Exit

Row Numbers

Cabin A

First Class Cabin

Cabin B

No Smoking Cabin

Exit

Exit

Service Centre

Cabin C

Exit

Exit

Cabin D

Exit

Exit

Washrooms

Air Canada Lockheed 1011

▶ 3. Look at the plan of the Lockheed 1011 jet plane. Troy sat in seat 23A. Was he closer to the front or the back? What cabins did he go through to visit the crew? How many exits are there? Why are there so many exits in the plane?

After leaving the plane, Mrs. Campbell and Troy found themselves inside the airport building. What a surprise! They had arrived at Canada's busiest air terminal. It was huge. Thousands of people were milling around. How could they possibly find their way in this confusing place?

Luckily, the flight attendant had shown them the way to the Customs and Immigration office. But then Troy and his mother wanted to collect their bags. Which way should they go? Uncle Ken was expecting them at the apartment when he finished work. How could they find a taxi to take them there?

These thoughts flashed through their minds. All of a sudden, Troy pointed. "Look at that sign, Mom. It's telling us where to get our bags."

"Good for you," his mother said. "Maybe we aren't lost after all!"

Troy and Mrs. Campbell followed the signs to the baggage area. Sure enough, the bags were waiting for them. The last time they had seen their bags was in Jamaica. Now they were here. It was almost like magic.

Before they went out to the taxi stand, Troy wanted something to drink. These symbols hung outside a row of shops. Which shop did Troy go into?

Every day, thousands of people from all over the world come to Canada. Most of them arrive at an airport. Canada is a strange new land to them. Many don't speak English or French. How do they find their way around?

Troy had found the easiest way to get around. He followed the symbols. They were simple and easy to understand. They gave information that many people wanted. These symbols are used in airports all over the world. What do you think they mean?

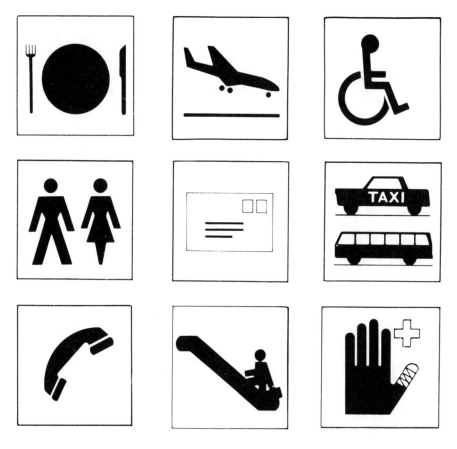

▶ 1. Draw some symbols that would help newcomers to find their way around your school. How many would be needed? Where should they be put?

▶ 2. Think about the stores in your community. Draw symbols that would tell people what is sold in some of the stores.

▶ 3. There are many symbols in every town. Look around your own community. What symbols are used? Draw some of them. Label them to say what each one means.

What might travellers want to know?

Workers at the Airport

Many people who work at the airport help travellers like Troy and his mother. It is important for them to speak a number of languages. All of the workers have special skills. Everyone works together to make the airport run smoothly.

Some workers can be heard but not seen.

There are people who work in little booths in the airport. Travellers come to them for help.

There are people who have other jobs to do but are always glad to help.

▶ 1. (a) What service is given by each person in the pictures?

    (b) How can a visitor tell that these people are airport workers?

▶ 2. Look in magazines and booklets for pictures of an airport and the people and things in it. Cut out the pictures. Glue them onto a sheet of paper. Give your page a title.

▶ 3. In one way your school is like an airport—people work together there, too. What people work in your school? What do they do?

HELP!

1. We are often in need of help. People, signs, and symbols can tell us where to get the help we need. What would you do if
    (a) you were lost in a store?
    (b) your car broke down on the highway?
    (c) you smelled smoke and no one else was home?

2. Sometimes *you* can be a helper. If you found a child crying on the street, how would you help? What questions would you ask?

9 Blackout

The Storm

It had been snowing all day. At first the snow came softly. Each flake was like a little kiss. Then the wind began. Coming home from school, Sarah had to turn her back against the storm. There was nothing soft about the snow now. It stung her cheeks.

A snowplough churned its way down the street. As it passed Sarah's house it piled snow across the driveway.

Sarah climbed over. She grabbed a snow shovel from the carport and started digging. Before long, her brother Jason joined her. Soon there was a wide gap in the snow.

"That's it." Sarah had to yell against the wind. "Mom can get the car in now."

Mrs. Stein was late getting home. Sarah decided to start supper. She turned on the stove and got out some potatoes to peel. Jason headed for the TV. He was supposed to help, but Sarah didn't care. She liked to work on her own.

Outside, snow drove against the kitchen window. The street lights were pale circles in the darkness. Sarah could see across the street, but only just. It was blowing a blizzard.

Suddenly the kitchen light dimmed, flickered—and went out. At the same time, the darkness outside was complete.

"Darn it! Right in the middle of my program!" There was no sound for a moment. Then Jason stood at the kitchen door. "Count Dracula strikes again!" he said.

"Don't be a nut. See if you can find your flashlight." Sarah felt her way along the kitchen counter. "I can't see a thing in this blackout," she said to herself. She opened a drawer and felt inside. Her fingertips touched tea towels, string, candle ends. The candles were just what she had been looking for—and matches. In no time she had two candles lit and set in a small dish.

There was a yell from Jason. "I've found my flashlight." A moment later he was back in the kitchen. "The battery's dead."

"Never mind. Here comes Mom."

▶ 1. Mrs. Stein was late getting home. How did Sarah and Jason show that they could look after themselves?

▶ 2. What did Sarah mean by "blackout"?

▶ 3. Why do you think the lights went out? What might have happened?

Suppertime

"Sorry I'm late," Mrs. Stein said as she came in. "Driving in that storm is terrible. Some trees have been blown down, and cars are stalled all over the road." She took off her coat. "You did well to find the candles. What's for supper?"

"Sandwiches," said Jason sadly. "The stove went off with the lights."

"Well, let's get a fire going. There are some logs in the wood box, Sarah. See what you can do. We can heat up some soup over the flames."

"The house is going to get cold, too. A fire will help keep us warm." Jason banged his flashlight against his hand as he spoke. The light came on. "Fantastic," he said. "It must have a loose connection."

"Come and give me a hand, Jason," Sarah called from the living room. "Bring the flashlight with you."

It was fun to have supper by the fire. Jason had bent a wire coat hanger so they could toast their sandwiches. They tasted wonderful. Near the fire it was cosy, but the rest of the house was cold. The wind roared outside.

There was a knock on the door. It was old Mr. Trant from next door. He wanted to borrow a flashlight or a candle. He smiled when he found the Steins sitting around the fire.

"Reminds me of when I was a boy," Mr. Trant said. "No electricity on the family farm then. I hope the power comes on soon, so I can make some supper."

Mrs. Stein got up. "Please sit down," she said. "Have supper with us."

▶ 1. When the lights and the stove went off, what else would go off?

▶ 2. Go through catalogues and magazines. Cut out pictures of things that need energy from electricity, oil, gasoline, coal, or wood. Group them by the fuel they use, and paste them in a pictograph.

▶ 3. How important is electricity to you? Find out this way. Make a chart of things that run by electricity. Use these headings.

In Our Classroom	In School	At Home

▶ 4. Mr. Trant's family had had to manage without electricity.
   (a) What would they have to do first thing on a winter morning that we don't have to do now?
   (b) What would they have to do as soon as it began to get dark?
   (c) What would they have to do last thing before going to bed?

▶ 5. (a) Have you ever gone camping or to a place that had no electricity? What did you use for lighting? cooking? heating?
   (b) Would you want to live without electricity all the time? Why, or why not?

Old Mr. Trant was glad to join the Steins. He didn't like living alone. He enjoyed sharing his thoughts and feelings with other people.

Mr. Trant finished his soup and a toasted cheese sandwich. "Thank you, Mrs. Stein. That was good." He settled back in his chair. "We sure are lucky people tonight," he said.

"Who's lucky?" Sarah didn't know what Mr. Trant meant.

"We are," said Jason. He was looking out the window. "Look at all that snow. Fantastic! There won't be any school tomorrow."

"Very funny." Mrs. Stein didn't really think it was funny. She had to get to work in the morning and she wanted her children in school. But Mr. Trant chuckled.

"I wasn't thinking of school," he said. "I was thinking we were lucky not to be out in this storm. All we have to do is stay in out of the cold. Sooner or later, the power will come on."

"How does that make us so lucky?" Jason asked. "Won't everyone be doing the same on a night like this?"

"No sir. Not everyone. A lot of people are out there in the blizzard."

"What people?" asked Sarah.

Mr. Trant thought for a minute. "I guess you could call them lifesavers," he answered.

▶ 1. (a) Why must some people live alone even though they don't want to?
   (b) How can neighbours help?

▶ 2. How would you like living by yourself? What would you like about it? What would you not like about it?

What are these people doing? Who are they? Why would Mr. Trant think of them as lifesavers?

The time passed quickly. Mr. Trant was glad to answer the Steins' questions about the old days on the farm. Sarah felt that they were getting to know their neighbour a lot better. Jason didn't even mention the TV programs he was missing.

They were playing the old game, "Twenty Questions", when all at once the lights came on. Music from the kitchen radio filled the house. Then an announcer spoke over the air.

"The community of Manston has been without power since six o'clock. Strong winds and driving snow are to blame. The hydro line came down near the power station at Loganville."

"We've been there," said Sarah. "We went on a school trip."

Jason hadn't been listening. "Been where?" he asked.

"To the power plant, the Loganville Generating Station."

"Oh, there. That was neat. We stood on the dam and watched the sailboats up the river."

"Well, it didn't take too long for the hydro crew to find the break and fix it." Mr. Trant stood up. "Hey, what's burning?"

Mrs. Stein ran to the kitchen. "My goodness. We must have left the stove turned on. But there's no harm done. It was just the hot burner you smelled."

"That's lucky, but you can't be too careful. It's good to get into the habit of switching things off. Saves energy, too."

"How about some dish-washing energy, then?"

"All right, Mrs. Stein. Show me where you keep the soap."

Mrs. Stein laughed. "I didn't mean you, Mr. Trant. I was talking to these rascals."

"We can all help. I'll wash. You dry." He tucked a tea towel into his belt and started to fill the sink with water.

▶ 1. What kind of energy was used by
    (a) the Steins and Mr. Trant, to do the dishes?
    (b) the sailboats on the river?
    (c) the power plant?

▶ 2. Give a name to each of these energy users and tell what kind of energy it uses.

▶ 3. What can you and your family do to save energy at home?

▶ 4. All of these people help to bring electricity to our homes. What do you think each person is doing?

▶ 5. (a) Make a note of all the safety rules you know about electricity.
   (b) Pick one rule and illustrate it on a poster.

▶ 6. (a) How do you and your family usually spend an evening at home?
   (b) Would you spend the evening differently if your home had no electricity? What would you like to do?
   (c) Do you think that people in the old days enjoyed themselves as much as we do now? Why, or why not?

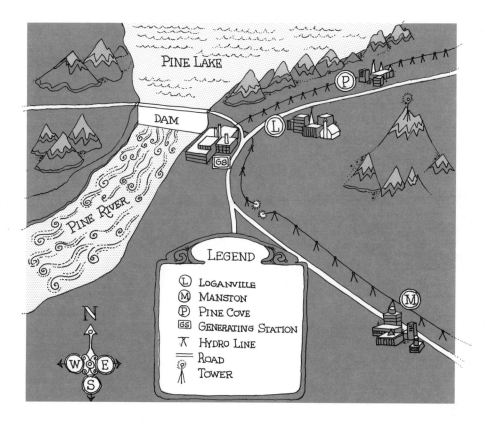

▶ 1. The towns of Loganville, Pine Cove, and Manston share the electric power generated at the Loganville power station.
   (a) Only Manston was blacked out. Why?
   (b) Why doesn't each town have its own power station?

▶ 2. (a) Was the power break north, south, east, or west of Manston?
   (b) Where was the break from Pine Cove?
   (c) Was the break closer to Manston or to Loganville?

▶ 3. (a) In what direction does the Pine River run? How can you tell?
   (b) What runs across the map east-west?

▶ 4. What is the highest point of land?

Communities Share Certain Things

There are many communities in the Vancouver area. The people who live in them share some services.

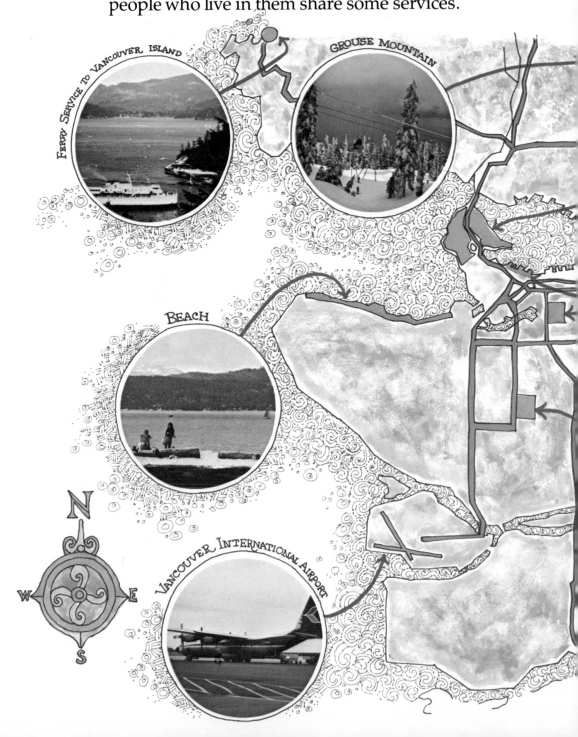

FERRY SERVICE TO VANCOUVER ISLAND

GROUSE MOUNTAIN

BEACH

VANCOUVER INTERNATIONAL AIRPORT

STANLEY PARK AQUARIUM

COLISEUM HOCKEY ARENA

PORT OF VANCOUVER

CN RAILWAY STATION

1221

N ELIZABETH PARK

▶ 1. What services in Vancouver help people to travel?

▶ 2. Where can people enjoy themselves? What can they do?

▶ 3. What services does your community share with other communities?

YOUR CLASSROOM

You spend a lot of time in your classroom. You and your class know it well, but other people don't. Many of them are interested in what you do in class and the people you work with. Tell them about your classroom in each of these ways.

1. Paint a picture.

2. Write a story.

3. Make a graph.

4. Draw a map. (Don't forget the legend.)

Make sure that the information is the same in all your work. For example, if you write that your classroom has four windows, make sure that your map shows only four windows.

Decide which of the four ways you will use to tell about
- the colours in your room,
- the furniture in your room,
- the people in your room,
- the way you feel about your room,
- the number of boys and girls in your room,
- where the boys and girls sit,
- what happens in your room.

This is a picture of Bob's classroom.

My Classroom

My classroom is warm and bright. It has lots chairs and desks. There is a craft centre with all sorts of stuff. There are two carpets on the floor. There are pictures up on the side board. I like my teacher because she is kind to us.

Bob wrote this story about his classroom.

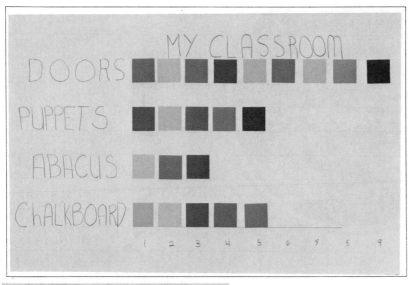

YOUR NEIGHBOURHOOD

What is your neighbourhood like?
Use a picture, a story, a graph, and a map to tell about your neighbourhood.

1. Where do you go?

2. Whom do you see?

3. Who talks to you?

4. What do you hear?

5. Whom would you like to meet?

6. What is growing?

7. What changes come with winter and with summer?

8. What do you like most?

9. How does it look in the rain?

Bob made a graph and a map of things in his classroom.

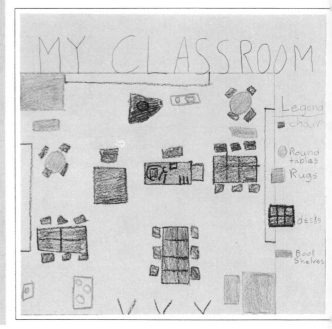

Yellowknife

Hamilton

Three Canadian Communities

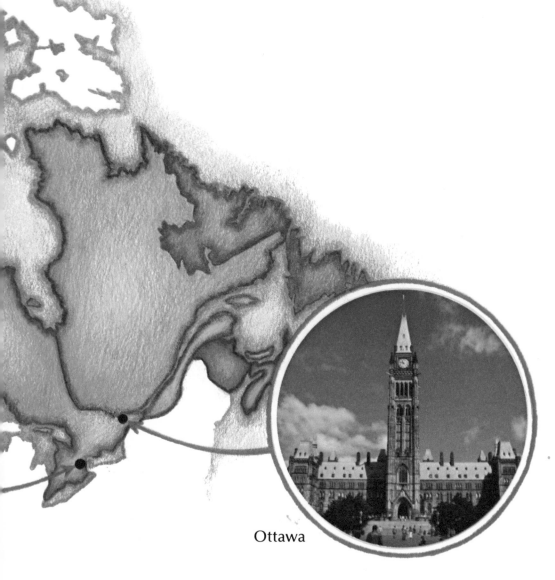

Ottawa

10 A Northern City: Yellowknife

Finding Treasure

"Gold! Gold! There's gold on the shores of Yellowknife Bay."

The year was 1934. The excited shout was made by a group of prospectors. They had been exploring the area.

These tough, brave men lived in the wilderness for

months at a time. Some lived alone, others in groups. Each man had a pick and a sample bag. He collected rock samples from different parts of the land. When the samples were brought back to camp they were tested to see what minerals were in them. The prospectors were searching for good supplies of minerals.

At Yellowknife Bay, their dreams came true. They had found gold.

▶ 1. What words would you use to describe this prospector?

▶ 2. What do his clothes tell you about the land around Yellowknife?

▶ 3. What types of transportation might this prospector have used to move about the land? Look at the pictures in this chapter. Now look at this list of words.
canoe
horse
train
jeep
snowshoes
aeroplane
car
dog team
snowmobile   Give reasons for your answer.

Mining the Gold

Finding the gold was only the start. Although the first samples had been found on the shore, most of the gold was deep in the ground. The only way to get it out was by digging a deep hole called a shaft. The miners used picks, shovels, and dynamite to get the job done. Less than two years after gold was found in Yellowknife Bay, the first mine was taking gold out of the ground.

Miners came from all over to work in the gold mine. It was a hard, dangerous life. Deep down, hundreds of metres below ground, the mine was cold, dark, and dusty.

▶ 1. How do the miners go down into the mine? How do they get out?

Gold ore.

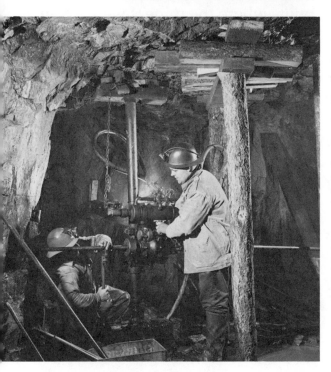

▶ 2. If you had to go down a mine, what would you wear on your feet? on your head? on your hands? Why? The photographs will help you answer.

▶ 3. What do we use gold for? Draw a picture of a piece of gold ore in the centre of a page. Around it, draw pictures of all the things you can think of that are made of gold. Label each picture.

When they came to work in the mines, the miners needed a place to live. There was nothing at Yellowknife Bay except trees, rocks, and northern lakes.

The mining company built camps. Wooden bunk-houses were made for the miners to sleep in. A large cookhouse was also built, where the miners were given good meals. All the miners lived in camp.

People who were not miners also came to Yellowknife Bay. They had to make their own places to live. Some brought tents with them and others built small frame shelters. These homes were very cold. When it rained, they leaked badly. A few people, who were a little better off, built log cabins. These were the first homes in the area. The town of Yellowknife had been founded.

Legend Door ⊢⟨ Window ⊢—⊢ Bunk ▦ Cupboard ▩

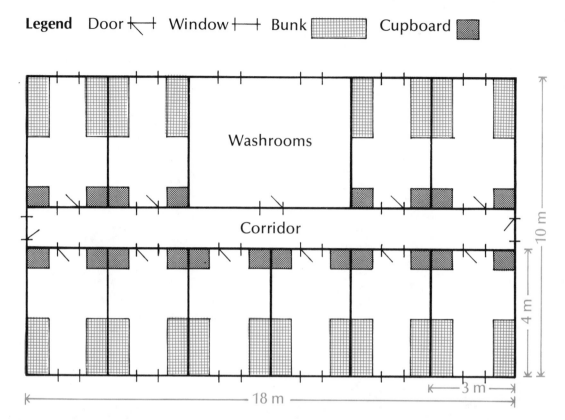

Washrooms

Corridor

10 m

4 m

3 m

18 m

Floor plan of a bunkhouse.

1. How wide are the rooms where the men slept?
2. How long is the bunkhouse?
3. If there were two bunks in each room, how many men could sleep in the bunkhouse?
4. What is the difference between a bunkhouse room and the room where you sleep?
5. Draw a floor plan of your bedroom.

▶ 1. (a) These people didn't work in the mine. What did they do?
   (b) Why do you think they came to Yellowknife?
   (c) What skills did they need to do their jobs?

▶ 2. Why did the miners who first came to Yellowknife not bring their families with them?

At first there was no running water for the people who lived in the town. Tom Doornbos, who arrived in Yellowknife with the other newcomers, carried water for the people. From a wooden yoke across his shoulders he hung a large bucket on each side. He carried the water to people's homes and sold it for 25¢ a pail. It was very hard work.

Tom Doornbos has seen Yellowknife grow from a little mining camp to a modern city.

► 1. Where did Tom get the fresh water?

► 2. What do you use fresh water for?

► 3. How long would a pail of water last in your home?

► 4. Where does the water in your home come from? How does it get to your taps?

Fire!

There was always a danger of fire in the new town. The tents and log cabins burned very easily. It took only a few sparks to send a shelter up in flames.

When a fire broke out, the first person to see it yelled "Fire!" There was no fire department or hoses, so every-one who heard the alarm came running to help. By standing in a long line, they formed a bucket brigade. They couldn't always save the burning home, but they did stop the fire from spreading to others in the town.

▶   1. How does the bucket brigade work?

▶   2. There are buckets for everyone. Why don't the people try to put out the fire on their own?

▶   3. What are some problems a bucket brigade might have?

▶   4. What fire protection is provided in your community?

A Growing Town

In the next few years, new mines were opened in the Yel-lowknife area. Many more people came to work there. Some brought their families with them. By 1942 Yel-lowknife was too crowded, and there was no land left on which to build. It became known as Old Town.

The citizens of Yellowknife had to look for new land. Nearby they found the perfect place. It was a wide, flat, sandy area. Soon new houses, schools, stores, hotels, and roads were built there.

Yellowknife, 1945.

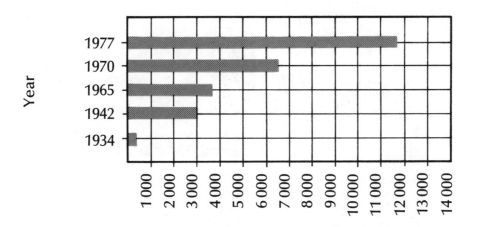

Population of Yellowknife

How many people lived in Yellowknife in 1942? In what year did the town suddenly get bigger? How many people lived in Yellowknife in 1977?

140 *People at Work*

All of these people live and work in Yellowknife now.

▶ 1. What are their jobs?

▶ 2. Which jobs were not there in the early days?

List the activities shown here, and write the temperature beside each.

▶ 1. In what seasons of the year do the activities shown in the pictures take place? How do you know?

▶ 2. What is the weather like in Yellowknife during the summer? during the winter?

▶ 3. Make a chart of the activities that take place in your community in each season of the year.

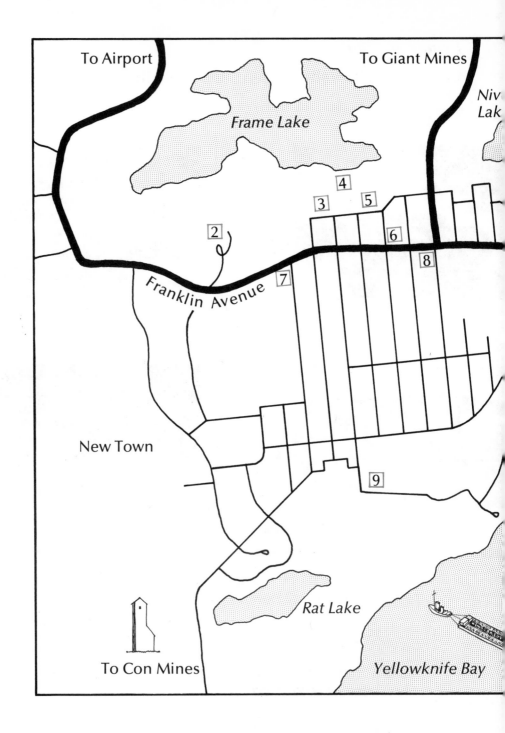

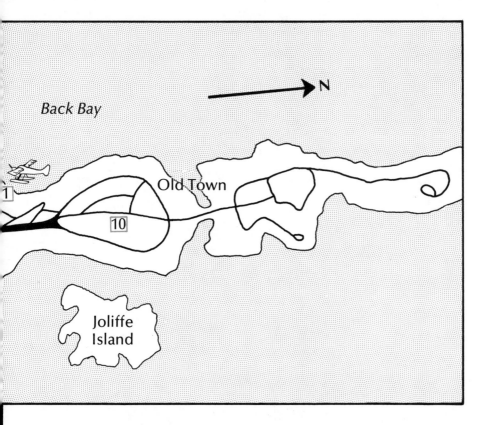

▶ 1. Why couldn't any more houses be built in Old Town?

▶ 2. Why was there a seaplane base in Old Town?

▶ 3. If you were going to live in Yellowknife, would you want to go to Old Town or the new town? Why?

▶ 4. How can you tell that many people have moved into Yellowknife during the last few years?

▶ 5. Locate these places on the map.

1	Seaplane Base	6	Post Office and Courthouse
2	Hospital	7	Y.W.C.A.
3	Arena and Curling Rink	8	Library
4	City Hall	9	Swimming Pool
5	R.C.M.P.	10	Pilot's Monument

Use the map of Yellowknife to help you find these places on the photograph.

Old Town   Yellowknife Bay
New Town   Back Bay
Joliffe Island   Frame Lake

LOOKING AT YOUR COMMUNITY

1. Where were the first homes and buildings constructed in your community? Where are the newer areas?

2. What helped your community to get started?

The stores in Yellowknife are like most other stores in Canada. They are full of different foods and supplies. People can buy anything from a pair of woollen gloves to a bag of apples.

There is a difference, though. All the goods cost much more than they do in other parts of Canada. There are no big farms or factories near Yellowknife. Almost everything that is sold in the stores is grown or made somewhere else. Some of these places are thousands of kilometres away.

Highways in the sky, on land, and on the water are like life lines to Yellowknife. Without them, the city could not exist.

▶ 1. What food is raised near your community?

▶ 2. What goods are made near you? What sort of factories are these goods made in?

▶ 3. How do food and manufactured goods get into stores in your community?

A Capital City

In 1967, on Canada's hundredth birthday, Yellowknife was named the capital of the Northwest Territories. This meant that the government of the Territories would be in Yellowknife. The people who worked for the government would live there. More families moved in. More houses, apartments, and office buildings went up. The city was growing again.

11 A Southern City: Hamilton

Many parts of Canada were opened up by settlers who were looking for land to farm. These pioneers travelled in different ways. The first ones to see the land at the western end of Lake Ontario arrived by boat. There were no roads through the forests then. The easiest way to travel was on the lakes and rivers.

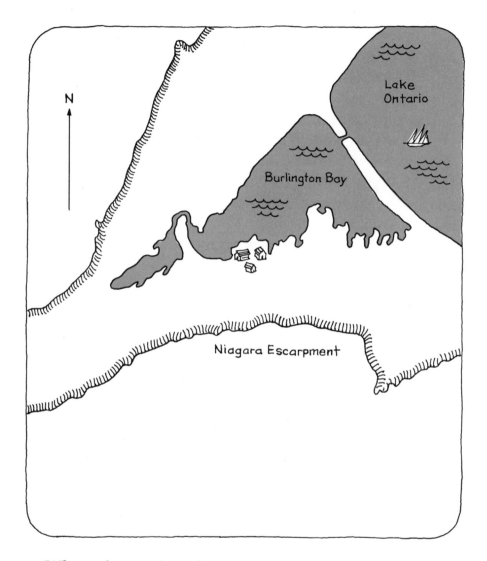

When the settlers found the land they wanted, the hard work began. Every member of the family helped in some way.

First, they had to chop down the trees. They used the logs to build their first small cabins. Then they ploughed the land around the tree stumps. A horse or an ox pulled the plough. When this was done, the settlers planted their first seeds. Later on, the stumps would be burned or pulled out. It took many years of hard work to clear the land.

The pioneer families grew most of their own food. Vegetables such as cabbages, potatoes, and turnips were grown on their farms. Most families kept some chickens, a few pigs, and a cow. And from fruit that grew wild nearby—raspberries, strawberries, and currants—they made tasty jams and pies.

As the years went by, more families moved to this area at the end of Lake Ontario. They came along narrow,

C.W. JEFFERYS

bumpy roads that had been cut through the bush. Their wagons were pulled by oxen. They brought with them everything they owned.

The soil in the area was good for farming. Soon, most of the land was being turned into farms.

▶   1. What tools were most important to the pioneers?

▶   2. Why was wood important to them?

▶   3. How may the settlers have helped one another?

▶   4. (a) Why did settlers choose the area at the western end of Lake Ontario?
      (b) What did they find there that they would not find in the Yellowknife area?

▶   5. Who settled first in your community? How did they get there?

▶   6. Why did the settlers choose your area?

▶   7. What was the land like when they first arrived? What is it like today?

▶   8. What crops did they grow?

The Mills

As more and more land was being farmed, mills were built nearby. They provided important services for the settlers. It was much easier to have the sawmill cut logs into planks than to do it by hand. The flour mill ground a farmer's grain into flour in no time.

A mill was always built beside a stream. The water flowing by supplied the power to run the mill.

Farmer brings grain to mill.

Farmer picks up sacks of flour from the mill.

Water in stream turns the water wheel.

Stones grind the grain into flour.

Water wheel makes the huge grindstones turn.

A flour mill. How was the flour used by the settlers? What foods today have flour in them?

The Town by the Bay

The people living on the farms in the area needed other services as well. The nearest towns were far away. It took a long time to get to them on the rough roads. To solve the problem, the settlers decided to build their own town. Then they could have the services they needed all together in their own area.

The land beside the bay was chosen. The town would be built beside one of the best harbours in Canada. It was a safe place for ships to stop. The people called the new town Hamilton, the name of the man who owned the land.

The first building to go up in the new town was the courthouse.

Beside the courthouse was the market place. Farmers from all over the district came to the market. There they sold the extra things they had grown or made on their farms. With the money they made, they bought other things they needed. Vegetables, fruit, chickens and eggs, cheese, butter, pickles, and many other things were bought and sold. The farmers' market in Hamilton is still used today.

▶ 1. How was the name of your town chosen?

▶ 2. What were the first buildings to provide services in your community?

▶ 3. Why were those buildings important? Are they still important?

▶ 4. Where is the nearest market to you? What can you buy there?

The citizens of the new town lived in fear of fire. Most of their buildings were made of wood. They had been built close together. A fire could quickly spread and burn down many buildings.

It was everyone's duty to help protect the town from fire. There were no fire hydrants. The houses did not have running water. Fire fighters had to carry water with them to the blaze.

When the men in the fire department heard the fire bell ring, they stopped whatever they were doing and ran to the fire station. They dragged a small hand pumper to the fire.

It was the law that each house had to have a bucket filled with water. Each house also had to have a ladder fixed to the roof. There was a fine for anyone who did not obey the fire laws.

► 1. What is happening at the fire in the picture at the top of the page? What are the people doing? How can you tell that the fire took place many years ago?

► 2. What is the difference between the old fire engines and those of today?

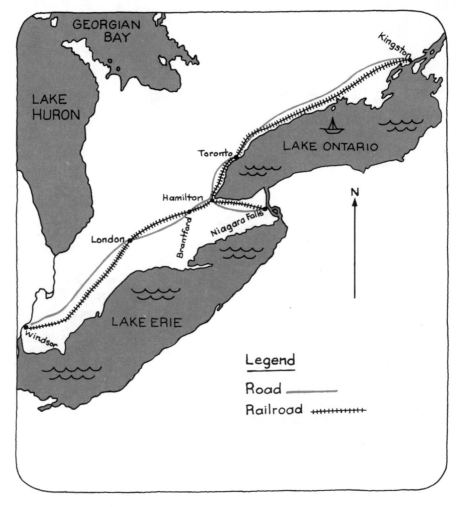

▶ 1. What route would you take to travel from Toronto to Niagara Falls by road? What towns would you pass through?

▶ 2. What route would you take to get from Niagara Falls to London by train? What towns would you pass through?

▶ 3. What route would you take to travel from Windsor to Kingston by ship? What ports could you stop at?

The pioneers couldn't go everywhere by boat. They needed roads, too. The first log and dirt roads around Hamilton were very rough. Travelling on them, on horseback or by horse and cart, was very slow. Later on, stagecoaches carried passengers to many towns. The coaches, too, were slow and bumpy. They often got stuck in the mud. When this happened, the passengers had to get out and push.

One day, a steam engine came to Hamilton. It was on its way to Windsor. Clouds of smoke puffed from its tall smokestack. It was pulling several long coaches. The people were excited. This was the first train to come to Hamilton. Everyone wanted to ride on it! From then on, the railway was important to the growing city.

Travel between Hamilton and other towns along the lakes was cheap and easy. There were many ships sailing on the lakes. They visited all the ports on Lake Ontario and Lake Erie. The ships carried many passengers to and from Hamilton. They also carried things to and from

the merchants and factories there. Like the railway, they helped to make Hamilton a good place to live and work. They, too, helped the town to grow.

▶ 1. (a) Why was the train a better way to travel than the stagecoach?
  (b) What could the train carry besides passengers?

▶ 2. Why would it be cheaper to travel by ship than by train?

▶ 3. How did people in early times get around the area where you live?

▶ 4. What is your favourite way of getting around? Why?

As the town of Hamilton grew, a community was being formed along the bay.

The ships sailing to Hamilton needed a place to tie up.

Docks were built so that the ships could be loaded and unloaded.

Warehouses were built to hold the goods carried by the ships.

People came to this part of the city. They worked on the docks and in the warehouses.

The workers built houses nearby. They wanted to be close to their jobs.

Merchants built stores in the community. They sold things to the people who lived and worked there.

This was only one of the communities that grew up within the city. All large towns are made up of different communities. Some are old, and some are new. Many are a mixture of both. The face of a town is changing all the time.

▶ Where do the people in your community work? How close are they to their jobs? How do they get to work?

Hamilton in 1845.

Hamilton in 1878.

▶ 1. Compare the pictures of Hamilton. How has the city changed?

▶ 2. Which is the oldest part of your town or the town nearest to where you live? Which is the newest part?

▶ 3. What buildings have been torn down in your town? Why? What was built in their place?

Hamilton in 1920.

Hamilton in 1978.

Hamilton is now a large city. Life there is much different from when the first pioneers came. It is no longer a small farming community. Through the years, changes have been taking place. Now there are many communities, and each one is important to life in Hamilton. Although people live in one community, there are reasons why they need the others.

3

4

5

9

10

▶ 1. Write the number of each photograph in which you see a part of the community
   (a) where people can enjoy themselves,
   (b) where people work,
   (c) that offers a service.

▶ 2. Now write the number of each photograph that shows something that is used
   (a) only by the people who live in the community,
   (b) by people from all over the city.

▶ 3. Compare your town to Hamilton as it is shown in these pictures. What is similar? What is different?

12 Ottawa: Our Nation's Capital

It was early in the day when the Martins reached Parliament Hill. They had left their motel right after breakfast. They didn't want to miss anything. This was their first visit to Ottawa.

Tracy and Peter were excited. They were in the capital of Canada! At home, the Martins had talked about the government.

"Remember when we voted in the last election?" Mrs. Martin asked. "The winner in our district was Mary Malone. She became our Member of Parliament—MP, for short. Mrs. Malone lives in Ottawa now. She helps to make the laws of Canada."

The Martins had come to Parliament Hill to see the Changing of the Guard.

"What a thrill!" thought Tracy. "I saw it once in a movie at school. But now I'm really here!"

Many other people were there, too, to see the famous ceremony. It was very crowded.

Tracy was eleven years old and quite tall for her age. She could see the parade grounds. Peter, three years younger, wasn't so lucky. He kept stretching to catch sight of the soldiers. All he could see was the back of the big man in front of him.

Peter's father saw the problem. "Would you like to sit on my shoulders for a while?" he asked.

"I sure would," said Peter with a grin. He climbed up. "Thanks."

The soldiers marched onto the grass led by a band. They wore bright red uniforms and tall, black, bearskin hats. What a picture they made!

When the parade ended, the people started to move away. The Martins were then able to look at the huge grey building in front of them. A red and white Canadian flag flew over the highest tower.

"I know what that place is," said Tracy. "It's the Parliament Building."

"You're right," replied Mrs. Martin. "That's where the Government of Canada meets. The building looks the same as when it was built over sixty years ago. I wonder if Mrs. Malone is there today."

People have always liked to visit Parliament Hill.

Many of them go inside the House of Commons to watch the Members of Parliament debate. The buildings may look the same as they did sixty years ago, but the way people dress and travel has changed.

▶ 1. How did the people in the picture travel in winter? How would they travel in summer?

▶ 2. How would you travel around Ottawa today, in winter? in summer?

▶ 3. What is different about the way the people dressed? Do you prefer the style of olden days or that of today? Why?

Before Peter had a chance to ask what they were doing next, Mrs. Martin spoke.

"Your dad and I have a surprise for you. We are going to meet Mrs. Malone in half an hour. When I knew we were coming to Ottawa, I decided to write her a letter. Since she is our Member of Parliament, we wanted to meet her."

"That's great," said Tracy. "She'll be able to tell us all about Parliament."

"Let's ask that Mountie how to get to her office," said Mr. Martin. An R.C.M.P. officer was standing at the top of the steps. Peter was already admiring the famous uniform. They went over to the officer, who gave them directions.

Mrs. Malone was pleased to see them. This was a good chance for her to show people from her home town where she worked and what she did.

"I spent three hours in the House of Commons yesterday," she told them. "We have so many problems to solve. The Prime Minister did most of the talking. We other MP's will get our chance today. By the end of the week we should be ready to vote on some new laws."

They chatted for a while. Then Mrs. Malone said, "Before you go, I'd like to show you around the House of Commons. And I thought you might like to visit the Royal Mint. I've arranged for you to have a tour this afternoon."

172   Members of Parliament come to Ottawa from every part of Canada. They have been elected by the voters in their home districts, or ridings. Each one belongs to a political party. The leader of the party that has the most MP's becomes the Prime Minister of Canada.

▶ 1. What is the name of your Member of Parliament?

▶ 2. What political party does your MP belong to?

▶ 3. What are the other major parties in Canada?

▶ 4. Who is the Prime Minister of Canada? Of what party is the Prime Minister the leader?

Every new law must be voted on in the House of Commons. If it is passed by the MP's, it must still be approved in the Senate. Together, the House of Commons and the Senate make up the Government of Canada.

The House of Commons.

The Senate.

▶ 1. What is the difference between a rule in your house and a law?

▶ 2. Who makes laws? Who makes the rules in your home?

▶ 3. Why must every new law be voted on?

▶ 4. Should you obey laws and rules that you don't like? Why?

▶ 5. What would life be like without rules in your home? without laws in our country?

The Martins came out of the Parliament Buildings into the bright sunshine. They decided to have lunch outside. Not far away was the Sparks Street Mall. It used to be a street with cars and buses on it. Now it is just for people to walk on, shop, and enjoy themselves.

After lunch the family looked at their map of Ottawa. They chose a route to the Royal Mint that they could walk.

It took them only a couple of minutes to reach the Rideau Canal. It was on their way to the Mint. Tracy leaned over the bridge and looked down.

"Hey, look at those boats," she said. "Imagine having boats in the middle of the city!"

"The Rideau Canal was built for shipping many years ago," her father replied. "But then ships got too big for it. It's mostly pleasure-boats that use it now."

"The canal is important to the people who live in Ottawa. They enjoy it all year round," added Mrs. Martin.

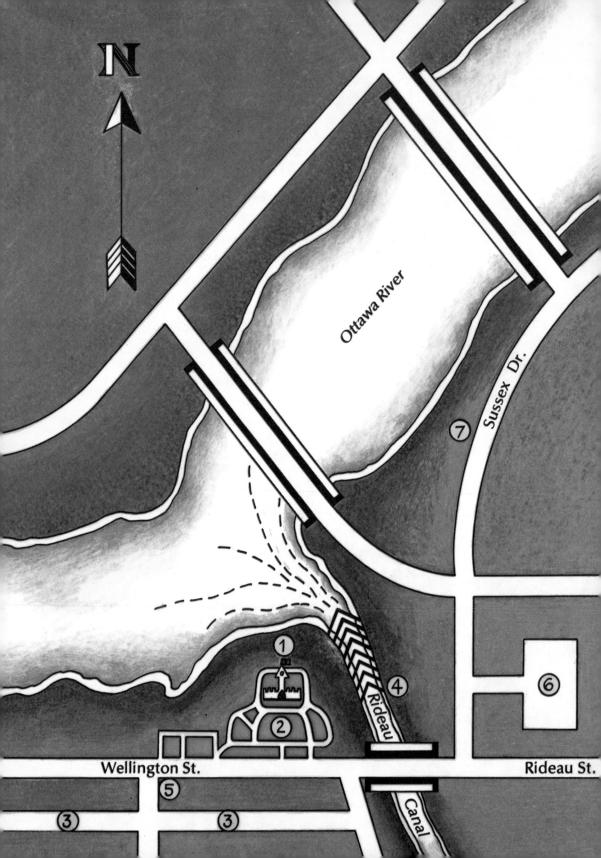

N

Ottawa River

Sussex Dr.

⑦

Rideau

④

①

②

⑥

Wellington St.

Rideau St.

⑤

③

③

Canal

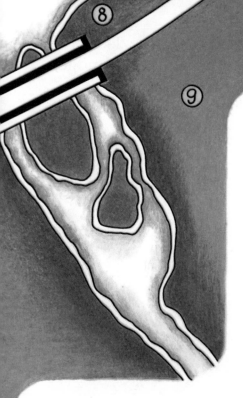

Legend

1 Parliament Hill

2 Centennial Flame

3 Sparks Street Mall

4 Rideau Locks

5 Bank of Canada

6 Byward Market

7 Royal Mint

8 Prime Minister's House

9 Rideau Hall

10 Embassies of Other Nations

▶ 1. The Martins want to walk from the Sparks Street Mall to the Royal Mint. What route will they take?

▶ 2. Which is closer to the Royal Mint, Parliament Hill or Rideau Hall?

▶ 3. Which is farther from the Byward Market, the Rideau Locks or the Centennial Flame?

▶ 4. What river does the Rideau Canal flow into? In what direction is it going?

▶ 5. What is the name of the road where the Prime Minister lives?

▶ 6. Every day, after the Changing of the Guard, the soldiers march to Rideau Hall. What route do you think they take?

Tracy was studying the map. She looked puzzled. "This map says there are locks on the other side of the bridge," she said. "What does a lock have to do with water?"

"Let's go over and have a look," suggested her mother.

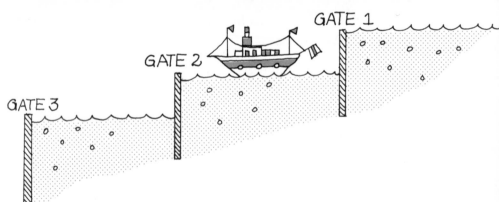

How many locks does a boat go through to get from the Rideau Canal down to the Ottawa River?

A strange sight met their eyes. The canal suddenly dropped down in steps to the river. There were boats floating on the steps. Mr. Martin explained that each of these steps was called a lock.

Here's how each lock works.

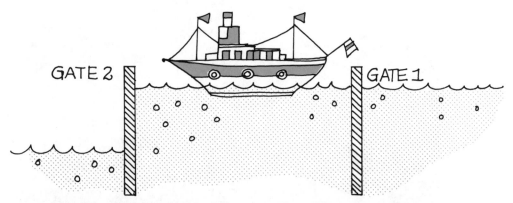

GATE 2   GATE 1

1 • THE BOAT IS STEERED INTO THE LOCK.
2 • BOTH GATES ARE CLOSED.

GATE 2   GATE 1

1 • THE WATER IS LET OUT OF THE LOCK.
2 • THE BOAT GOES DOWN WITH THE WATER.
3 • GATE 2 IS OPENED AND THE BOAT LEAVES THE LOCK.

▶ Can a boat travel from the Ottawa River *up* the Rideau Canal? How?

At the Royal Mint, the Martins found a guide waiting for them. He told them they were going to see money being made. The children were relieved. When they first saw the building they thought it was a prison.

The guide took them into a busy, noisy factory. Metal was being melted. Shiny new coins were coming out of machines. The testing room was much quieter. Here the new coins were weighed, checked over, and counted. When all this was done, the coins were poured into white canvas bags. The bags would be taken from here to a safe vault. They would be kept there until they were needed by the government's bank, the Bank of Canada.

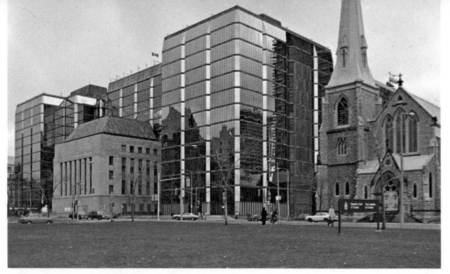

The Bank of Canada, Ottawa.

▶ 1. How many different Canadian coins are there up to $1.00? Make a rubbing of each coin.

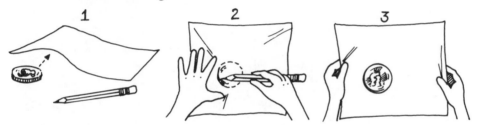

▶ 2. If you had one coin of each value, how much would they add up to?

▶ 3. Collect several pennies from other children in the class. Put them in order from the oldest to the newest.
　(a) When was the oldest coin minted? How old is it?
　(b) When was the newest coin minted? How old is it?

▶ 4. Why is it that only the government can make coins and paper money in Canada?

▶ 5. Whose picture is on every Canadian coin? Why?

▶ 6. What route would a truck take to go from the Mint to the Bank of Canada?

It had been an interesting day for the Martins. And it wasn't over yet.

"Let's go around the city and look at some of the important buildings," said Mrs. Martin. "There are still so many to see."

"A good idea," her husband said. "But let's drive in the car. It's too far to walk."

"And can we please eat first?" begged Peter. "I'm starved!"

The home of the Prime Minister is owned by the people of Canada. Every new Prime Minister moves into this house at 24 Sussex Drive.

The Governor General of Canada, who represents the Queen, lives at Rideau Hall. When important visitors come to Canada they often stay at this beautiful house.

In Ottawa there are many big houses called embassies. Ambassadors, who represent other countries, live in them. Ambassadors are sent to Ottawa because it is the capital of Canada.

A large number of people who live in Ottawa work for the government. Many of them are called civil servants. Their office buildings are located all through the city.

▶ 1. Look back at the pictures and map in this chapter. What place in Ottawa would you most like to visit? Why?

▶ 2. A friend who has never been in your area is coming to visit you. What is the most interesting place to take your friend? Why do you think so?

Acknowledgments

Grateful acknowledgment is made to those who provided the drawings and photographs on the pages listed below.

Drawings
Brenda Clark: 17-30, 128-43; Sylvie Daigneault: 65-9, 90-100, 168-81; Helen Fox: 2-14, 74-88, 147; Lorraine LeCamp: 46-60, 161; Colette MacNeil: 32-44, 102-25.

Photographs
Air Canada: 110; Archives of Ontario: 154, 155, 156 (left), 157 (lower left), 163 (upper); Department of Information, Government of the Northwest Territories: 128 (upper), 130, 132, 133 (right, lower), 137, 140 (bottom left, bottom right Lorne Smith, and centre right), 141, 144-5, 146 (top); Ford Motor Company of Canada Ltd.: 146 (lower left); Phil Goodwin: 12 (lower), 50 (upper right), 97; Greater Vancouver Convention & Visitors Bureau: 124-5 (beach, ferry service, Stanley Park, Coliseum, Port of Vancouver); Barry Griffiths: 1, 12 (upper left and right), 41 (all except fire hall), 42, 45, 50 (upper left), 62, 63, 70, 71, 73, 75, 76, 77 (upper), 78, 80, 84, 89, 124-5 (airport, railway station), 126 (left), 129, 146 (cattle), 148, 163 (lower), 164-5 (upper row, middle; bottom row, last three photos on right), 166, 168; Gulfstream Public School, North York, Ont.: 126 (right), 127; Head of the Lake Historical Society, Hamilton: 160 (lower); Metropolitan Toronto Library Board: 150, 160 (upper), 162; Miller Services Ltd.: 34, 50 (lower), 131; National Capital Commission: 173 (right), 174, 175, 182, 183, 184; NFB Photothèque ONF: 173 (left) *68-3941K*, 180 *79-1563Kb*, 181 *79-1562Kb*; Ontario Hydro: 122; Ontario Ministry of Agriculture and Food: 146 (lower right); Ontario Ministry of Industry and Tourism: 128 (lower), 140 (upper left and right), 164-5 (top row, first two and last two; bottom row, first two), 167, 178; Karlene Plummer (Ken Jansz): 77 (lower); Prince of Wales Northern Heritage Centre, Yellowknife: 134, 135, 136, 139; Public Archives of Canada, Ottawa: 151, 152, 156 (right), 157 (upper) *C-62587*, 159 *C-69849*, 169 *C-82886*; Royal Ontario Museum: 133 (upper left); Janet Skodyn (Basil Skodyn): 124-5 (Grouse Mt., Queen Elizabeth Park); Toronto Fire Department: 41 (fire hall), 86, 157 (lower right); Transport Canada: 107, 108, 109, 111, 112.

08 18 28 38 48 58 68 78 88 BP 9 8 7 6 5 4 3 2 1